keehkaapiišamenki:
A History of the Allotment of Miami Lands
in Indian Territory

keehkaapiišamenki:
A History of the Allotment of Miami Lands in Indian Territory

History text by George Ironstrack
Allottee biographies by Meghan Dorey
Allotment map by Bradford Kasberg

Produced by the Miami Tribe of Oklahoma Cultural Resources Office with funding from the National Historic Preservation Fund, Grant #40-11-NA-4054.

Other grant related productions include a printed map of the Miami allotment lands and online resources located at http://www.myaamionki.org.

Cover design and layout by Julie Olds
Cultural Resources Officer, Miami Tribe of Oklahoma

kweehsitoolaanki

With deepest respect the Miami Nation dedicates this publication to the memory of our beloved relative, elder and historian, the late Clarence Eugene "Gene" Hayward. Gene was a quiet and humble soul who dedicated his latter years to personal research into the history of the Miami people from their arrival in Kansas, following the 1846 removal, until their departure in the early 1870's. His research culminated in the publication titled "The Lost Years: Miami Indians in Kansas", copyrighted in 2010.

With this publication we acknowledge and remember the Myaamia people who chose to retain their citizenship, following the requirements of the 1867 treaty, by choosing to remove from their Kansas homelands to the Indian Territory in the early 1870s. Had it not been for their collective decision to hold tight to their identity as Miami citizens, and endure another period of reestablishment, the Miami would not exist as a sovereign Nation today. Our hearts must be forever grateful for their sacrifices.

Table of Contents

Preface

This book takes an honored place in the series of heritage preservation publications created by the Miami Tribe of Oklahoma. Following "myaamiaki aancihsaaciki: A Cultural Exploration of the Myaamia Removal Route", published in 2011, Myaamia youth researching our traditional kinship system, began to seek more knowledge of the history of their immediate ancestors and their stories of removal. This, coupled with the need to create an accurate map of our alloted lands, led the Cultural Resources team to develop this unique, grant-funded project. Prior to this research, no comprehensive written history of our ancestors' arrival and settlement in the Indian Territory was available. While this written documentation was absent, an erroneous map, created by a non-Tribal citizen, was well circulated and accepted as truth, both by historians and our own community.

The project team included historians, linguists, archivists, cultural leaders, Natural and Cultural Resource specialists, a web developer and a mapping expert. Members of the project team scoured archival repositories in Washington, D.C., Ft. Worth, TX, Kansas City, MO and Oklahoma City, OK and delivered the data to our research workhorse, Myaamia historian George Ironstrack. His thoughtful, informed text aptly tells the collective story of our history through removal from our Kansas homeland to the Indian Territory and the ensuing years of settlement, allotment, and assimilation tactics. Meghan Dorey, Director of the Myaamia Heritage Museum & Archive, compiled a database of allotment records, collected photographs of allottees and interviewed descendants to write the biographical sketches. The mapping team reviewed original land records, researched surveyors' journals, and utilized modern GIS/GPS technologies to generate the most accurate model of our allotment area.

We have respectfully worked to create a tool for our community in our quest to understand our history as a people and how that path brought us to this land we call myaamionki noošonke siipionki - the Myaamia lands near the Neosho River. We, as a team, have been humbled by our experiences and the knowledge gained in this project. We want our Myaamia relatives to know that we entered this project seeking answers to many serious questions, and while we were able to find some answers, many still elude us. This work, in seeking

Preface

knowledge, is an ever looping circle of asking questions to gain knowledge, which in turn leads us to be able to ask more questions. We have only just begun. This book represents our first step in this expansive and complex subject, and we are grateful to take this opportunity to take the responsibility to share what we have learned with our people. We ask our relations to view and use, this book as the tool it is intended to be. We encourage you to join with us in seeking knowledge, documents, photos and other pertinent pieces that will help us expand our understanding and further tell this story.

We extend respect and appreciation from the Cultural Resources Team to the Myaamia Nation. It is our great honor to serve you.

Julie Olds
Cultural Resources Officer

Meghan Dorey
Director, Myaamia Heritage Museum & Archive

Acknowledgments

The Cultural Resources Office of the Miami Tribe of Oklahoma extends appreciation and respect to the following individuals, without whose expertise this publication would not have been possible:

The Chief and Business Committee of the Miami Tribe of Oklahoma, for their personal commitments to our heritage preservation efforts and empowering us to seek and share this knowledge with our people.

To the National Park Service, National Historic Preservation Fund, for providing opportunities to us, and other Nations, working to maintain identity and culture.

To Myaamia Center Director Daryl Baldwin, and staff members David Costa and George Ironstrack for their invaluable contributions in language review and extensive historic research.

To Anna McKibben, our initial grant writer, for putting our request to paper and submitting it for funding.

To Dr. John Bowes and Dr. Cameron Shriver, for their time committed in peer review and comment.

To our esteemed elder George Strack, for review and comment.

To Myaamia genealogist John Bickers, for his assistance and research on allottee Myaamia names.

To Bradford Kasberg, for creating the new allotment map for this project.

To Meghan Dorey, our archivist, historian, researcher, and museum professional whose expertise led to assembling the personal information and photos on each allottee.

To Rise Proctor of the Quapaw Tribe, for providing images of Shapp family members.

To our elder Sammye Leonard Darling, whose personal database of family history information served as a framework on which to build.

Introduction

In 1884, a Myaamia (Miami Indian) family participated in the second forced removal of the Miami Nation from Kansas to Indian Territory.[1] The Palmer family had built a life for themselves in Kansas, but in order to remain a part of their nation, they had to move to Indian Territory. In the spring of that year, Elizabeth Palmer, her husband Jim, and her young son Harley arrived on their new lands within the combined Miami and Peoria Reservation in the northeast corner of Indian Territory. Their nation had purchased an undivided interest in the reservation that would give members a new place upon which to rebuild their lives. Elizabeth recalled that on behalf of the tribe, "Chief Richardville arranged and bought for the Miamis sufficient land from the Peorias for each [member] of the tribe living in Kansas to have 200 acres each." This new land lay "west and south of the Quapaws and west of the Peorias."

Elizabeth remembered that during that first spring she took Harley with her to live in Baxter Springs, which was the nearest town, while Jim began farming and building a new home for the family on land selected by the family. As soon as the weather warmed, Elizabeth took Harley and moved out into a large tent that Jim had put up just east of Tar Creek. At that time, the only other structure was "a large cook shed" that Jim "erected by placing posts in the ground and a support through the middle from which the boards sloped each way."

Harley recalled that in "those days this whole country was a great prairie." There were few fences, but cattlemen "were continually driving and grazing cattle" all over the Miami and Peoria Reservation. One story of that early chaotic period stuck with both Elizabeth and Harley. "Mother and I were alone at the tent one day," Harley recounted, and "when looking up we saw a wild steer headed straight towards us. She quickly set me up on a salt barrel that was sitting at one of the posts of the cook shed. She followed me on the barrel and then lifted me to the roof and followed me, and there we remained until those who were trailing the steer arrived and drove him away." Elizabeth recalled that the cattlemen did come by and offer their apologies. However, the danger of the situation convinced Elizabeth to move with Harley into a rental property until Jim finished the construction of the family's new house.[2]

Elizabeth and Harley Palmer's stories of the first years of the Miami Nation in Indian Territory paint a beautiful but stark picture. Their stories

Introduction

hint at the challenges facing their tribal nation after the end of the American Civil War. To remain a nation, they were forced to leave the Waapankiaakami (LaCygne River Valley) in eastern Kansas, a place that had been their home for less than forty years following the heart-wrenching forced removal of 1846.

In order to survive as a nation, the Miami Nation and its citizens were forced to remove to Indian Territory. On their lands along the Noošonke Siipiiwi (Neosho River) they made a new collective home. For nearly twenty years, the Miami Nation and its citizens lived on a shared reservation that was the collective property of the nation. In the 1890s, the nation's relationship to its home was altered in dramatic fashion through allotment: the formal legal division of collective lands into individually held property. The Miami Nation hoped that this transformation would help their people thrive again. Conversely, the government of the United States hoped that allotment would lead to the eventual dissolution of the Miami Nation as a sovereign government.[3] Allotment, it was hoped, would finish what the U.S. started all those years ago on the battlefields of the Wabash River Valley: the complete elimination of tribes from within the boundaries of the United States. In the end, neither group got what they expected.

What follows is *A History of the Allotment of Miami Lands in Indian Territory*. It has been a difficult topic to research and remains a challenging story to tell. However, we hope that by telling this story from the perspective of our nation, we will empower ourselves to think differently about who we were, who we are, and who we will be. Within this history there are powerful lessons for us to learn about how we treat our collective tribally-owned lands and our privately held land. Both are necessary, perhaps even essential, for our tribal nation to continue to thrive. But we must also work to educate ourselves about the differences between tribal lands and individual lands and to collectively recognize the relative importance of each to our continuance as a tribal nation and as Myaamia people.

This text is broken into two parts. Part I is a narrative history of the allotment of the lands of the Miami Tribe of Oklahoma. It begins with an overview of the early history of the Miami Nation, looks at the difficult transition from Kansas to Indian Territory (Oklahoma), and finishes with an examination of the allotment of the Miami Nation's reserved lands.

Part II presents short biographies of each tribal member who received an allotment in Indian Territory (often referred to as an allottee). Many years of family history researched by several people have contributed to these biographies. Much of the information presented has been culled from tribal rolls, land patents, newspaper articles, and many other primary archival documents. Almost all the photos included in this publication were contributed by family members of the allottees, for which we must say, "neewe!"

As records become available for research and we continue to learn about the tribal community at the time of allotment, details about these individual tribal members may change. If you have information that contradicts or expands on what is published here, we encourage you to contact the Myaamia Heritage Museum & Archive and share, so that our knowledge of our communal history can be better understood.

We must also note that these biographies profile only a section of the Myaamia community at this point in history. There were several other concentrations of Myaamia people in Kansas, Indiana, and even in Indian Territory that did not receive allotments with the Miami Nation. The life stories of these people are just as important and interesting as the Myaamia allottees presented here and may be addressed in future publications.

After reading through each of the sixty-six biographies, we hope it is apparent that the paths to allotment were varied throughout the Myaamia community. It is only by considering these varied paths that we can draw conclusions about the overall process of tribal allotment.

For many years, the standard reference map for Miami allotment lands has been "Indian Allotment Map, Ottawa County, Oklahoma," compiled by John L. Speer, the Ottawa County Surveyor from 1917 to 1944. This map shows all original allotments in Ottawa County for each of the area tribes, and notes all mine sites as well. In the area of Miami and Peoria allotments, there was no way to distinguish which tribe the allottee belonged to without returning to the original records, and there were several errors in both spelling and boundaries. One of the primary objectives of this research project was to re-create this map as a better tool for the needs of the Miami Nation and its citizens. The first step toward complet-

Introduction

ing this goal was digitizing the existing oversize map and then checking all Miami allotments against the original allotment register. Adding layers such as current town boundaries, roads, and landmarks assist in readily locating the allotments. As shown in the map, each of the 66 allottees received 200 acres of land. Some chose to have 160-acre homesteads with a 40-acre plot farther away for timber or water access, and others had a contiguous tract of the full 200 acres. Overall, we hope this map will not only help citizens identify where their direct family ancestors may have lived, but also help provide an understanding of the greater Myaamia community of the time.

Notes

1. The legal title of the nation is the "Miami Tribe of Oklahoma," and this publication will use that title when referencing the reorganization of the nation in 1939 and its current form. Throughout time, Myaamia communities have described themselves using many different terms in Myaamiaataweenki (the Myaamia language), French, and English. From the 1800s to the present day, Myaamia people have often referred to their nation as the Miami Nation. Throughout most of the publication, the term "Miami Nation" is used as a reflection of the language of the 1800s and to highlight the entity's unique sovereign status. This status existed prior to European arrival in North America and will hopefully continue forward for generations uncounted.

2. "Elizabeth Lindsey Palmer Interview," Indian-Pioneer Papers, The University of Oklahoma Western History Collections (https://digital.libraries.ou.edu/whc/pioneer/ accessed on October 4, 2012), 3-5. "H.T. Palmer Interview," Indian-Pioneer Papers, The University of Oklahoma Western History Collections (https://digital.libraries.ou.edu/whc/pioneer/ accessed on October 4, 2012), 1-4.

3. Chang argues, "The creation of private property simultaneously extended and masked the reach of state power." see David A. Chang, "Enclosures of Land and Sovereignty: the Allotment of American Indian Lands," Radical History Review, Issue 109 (Winter 2011), 109. The Dawes Act purported to extend U.S. citizenship over allottees, thereby removing citizens from the tribal nation, see Section 6 of Dawes Act. Otis quotes Senator Dawes as stating that allotment would serve as a "self-acting machine," which would start by eliminating the reservations and lead to the complete dissolution of the government to government relationship because all the Indians would become citizens of the United States. D.S. Otis and Francis Paul Prucha (ed.), The Dawes Act and the Allotment of Indian Lands (Norman: University of Oklahoma Press, 1973), 57-59. The most comprehensive history of United States policy regarding tribal nations and allotment is Frederick E. Hoxie, A Final Promise: The Campaign to Assimilate the Indians, 1880-1920 (Lincoln: University of Nebraska Press, 1984).

Part I - A History of the Allotment of Miami Lands in Indian Territory

Part I - A History of the Allotment of Miami Lands in Indian Territory

As a small tribal nation, the Miami Tribe of Oklahoma's experience with allotment has been like navigating a canoe through dangerous waters. Our people and their leaders have been continually challenged with the task of weaving their community through violent waves that threaten to sink our collective mihsooli (canoe). This experience has required our community to acknowledge that we have very little control over our broader environment. We recognized in our past and continue to recognize today that we must adjust our course in response to the forces raging around us, or we risk being overwhelmed. We have preserved our distinct identity as a tribal nation by carefully and thoughtfully changing the direction of our community mihsooli. The history of the Miami Nation's experience with allotment is instructive about the harm done when we lose much of the control and awareness of changes taking place within our community.

For over two hundred years, the Miami Tribe has faced forces that sought to divide our land and people. The struggle to navigate these destructive forces came to define the experience of the nation beginning with our first forced removal. It was in Kansas and four decades later in Oklahoma, that the nation faced the allotment of the collectively held national land base. Allotment - the legal division of collective land into individually owned property - nearly succeeded where wars and removal failed. But our people and our nation endured. What follows is a history of the allotment of our national lands in Indian Territory. This story recounts the difficult course we have been forced to navigate, but it also demonstrates that with increased awareness can come a good measure of increased control over our community mihsooli (canoe) and that no group or individual possesses the strength to wrench away control of our mihsooli as long as we continue to fiercely paddle together.

The Land and the People Before 1846

The historic homelands of the Miami Tribe of Oklahoma include land that eventually became the states of Indiana, Illinois, the western half of

A History of the Allotment of Miami Lands in Indian Territory

Ohio, and parts of southern Wisconsin and southern Michigan. The Miami, or Myaamia, were originally a village-centered people with six large villages and many smaller communities. The six large villages were Kiihkayonki (Ft. Wayne, IN), Kineepikwameekwa Siipiiwi (near Logansport, IN), Kiteepihkwani Siipiiwi (Lafayette, IN), Waayaahtanonki (south of Lafayette, IN), Peeyankihšia (near Cayuga, IN), and Aciipihkahkionki (near Vincennes, IN). Historically, all of these villages shared the same language and culture. They also shared a broad and loose political identity. Each village was relatively independent, but all Myaamia villages would come together to negotiate major issues around war, peace, and the sharing of essential resources.

These six semi-permanent Myaamia agricultural villages centered on the northern Wabash River and its tributaries, an area often referred to as the Miami Nation's heartlands. The rest of the homelands described above were utilized for hunting and gathering. All of the hunting and gathering grounds were negotiated and shared among the tribes of the lower Great Lakes, namely the Peoria, Kaskaskia, Wyandot, Ottawa, Potawatomi, Ojibwe, Shawnee, Seneca, Kickapoo, and Delaware. All of these communities have a deep history of negotiating for resources as neighbors and extended kin.

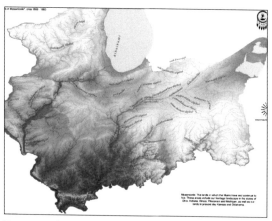

Riverine map of Myaamionki by Brett Governanti and Joshua Sutterfield. A larger image of this map can be found on page 44.

The Land and the People Before 1846

Through the 1600s and 1700s the Myaamia experienced many disruptions resulting from the arrival of Europeans in North America. Disease, trade, and increased warfare all had, at least in part, a negative impact on Myaamia communities. Yet, after each of these disruptions they were able to adapt, change, and reestablish an internal order based on their own cultural traditions. This changed rapidly with the end of the American Revolution and the eruption of sustained warfare (1784-1794) between the Myaamia and the newly-born United States of America.

In 1795, the Miami Nation signed the first of thirteen treaties with the United States.[1] Through these treaties, the Miami were forced to relinquish their homelands, which would eventually become the states of Indiana and Ohio, in exchange for annuity payments. These payments included goods, services, and money. Additionally, the terms of many of these treaties reserved land for individuals or families from the larger collective land cessions. Through this process, the Miami Nation struggled to rebuild an economy based in part on annuities, hunting, and farming on shared reservation land and individual or family lands with restricted patents. These restricted titles usually protected the land from sale for a set period of time. When sales did occur, they were supposed to require presidential approval.

By the late 1830s, most of the traditional Myaamia homelands had been ceded to the United States. Collectively, the Miami Nation maintained control over the Great Miami Reserve, which contained over 700,000 acres in northern Indiana.[2] Individually, families owned many small parcels of land along the Waapaahšiki Siipiiwi and its feeder streams. These parcels were concentrated between the cities of Logansport and Fort Wayne, Indiana. The United States had worked hard to divide Myaamia people from each other and from their land, and in many ways they were successful.

As a result of these changes, the treaty process fragmented the broad and loose confederation of Myaamia-speaking villages into at least three political entities. Along the northern Wabash, from the Kineepikwameekwa Siipiiwi (Eel River) to the headwaters of the Taawaawa Siipiiwi (Maumee River), communities unified to form the Miami Nation. The communities from

A History of the Allotment of Miami Lands in Indian Territory

Waayaahtanonki formed the Wea Tribe, and the Peeyankihšia villages from the area around Aciipihkahkionki (Vincennes, Indiana) joined to form the Piankashaw Tribe.

In 1830, the United States passed the Indian Removal Act and increased pressure on all tribes to move west of the Mississippi. In 1840, after ten years of resistance and for reasons that are not entirely clear, the Miami Nation agreed on paper to remove west of the Mississippi and relinquish their last reservation in Indiana in exchange for 500,000 acres in the Unorganized Indian Territory. Shortly after signing the treaty, Miami Nation leaders began work to delay or stop the removal while at the same time individual Myaamia families found ways to gain official exemption from removal.

All attempts at resistance came to an end in 1846, when federal troops were called to northern Indiana to begin the forced removal of the Miami Nation. By 1846, over 150 individual Miami had gained the right to receive their annuity payments in Indiana. This right was understood to make those families exempt from the removal. Tragically, this left over 300 Miami subject to removal many of whom were forcibly relocated to holding camps in Peru and Fort Wayne. In October of 1846, the Miami Nation began their forced removal via the canal and river systems of the Midwest. In November of 1846, with winter fast approaching, the Miami Nation arrived on the 324,976 acres that had been set aside in the Unorganized Indian Territory. This was over 175,000 acres less than what they had been promised by treaty, but the Miami Nation did not learn of the discrepancy until much later. The nation was partially compensated for this gross negligence in the twentieth century.[3]

As a fractured community, Myaamiaki (Miami people) faced one of the most challenging winters in their history in 1846-47. The Miami Nation rebuilt itself in the West through the labor of the 300 Myaamiaki who endured the forced removal. In the Wabash River Valley and southern Michigan, over 150 Myaamiaki struggled to maintain their individual families who were increasingly surrounded by (at times hostile) American settlers. Many of these families were officially exempted from removal, but some had fled from the soldiers and hidden away with Potawatomi relatives to the north. In both cases, citizens of the Miami Nation in the West saw these eastern Myaamiaki as residing outside of their tribal nation and lacking most of the political and legal protections maintained by their nation in the west. For a time, these absent citizens could regain these protections by moving west and rejoining their kin within the Miami Nation's shared land base.[4]

The Land and the People in Kansas (1846-1873)

Following the 1846 forced removal, the Miami Nation worked to reestablish itself within a new national land base: a reservation of approximately 325,000 acres near the Waapankiaakami (Marais des Cygnes River) in the Unorganized Indian Territory. From within its new national boundaries, the Miami Nation soon faced the renewal of pressure from the government of the United States to relinquish part or all of their governmental, geographic, and communal integrity. Despite these pressures, the nation maintained itself and the communal mihsooli was prepared for the cascading waters that threatened to drown the nation in late 1860s and early 1870s.[5]

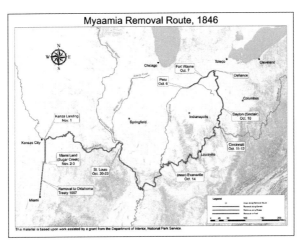

Map depicting the removal route of the Miami Nation in the fall of 1846. A larger image of this map is located on page 45.

A History of the Allotment of Miami Lands in Indian Territory

Upon arrival in their new home, the Miami Nation once again found themselves neighbors with many of the tribes with whom they shared their historic homelands. Directly to the nation's north were the reservations of the Wea, Piankashaw, Peoria and Kaskaskia. These four nations and the Miami Nation shared a language in common, had similar cultures, similar historical experiences, and in the case of the Wea and Piankashaw, a long history of intermarriage. These communities had become isolated from each other in the 1820s, but as extended kin they quickly renewed and revitalized their connections in the 1840s.

Initially, the Miami Nation's focus was on surviving a difficult winter and rebuilding their homes within their new national boundaries.[6] This was not easy, and the early years along the Waapankiaakami were defined by an intense struggle for physical survival. Slowly, the nation began to stabilize and grow again. As stability returned, so too did legal and political threats to the nation's continuance.

The first threat, which was a familiar one to the Miami Nation, was the return of the United States' quest to diminish and eventually eliminate the nation's land base. In 1854, the United States passed the Kansas-Nebraska Act, which transformed the lands around the Miami National Reservation into Kansas Territory. By establishing that the voting public would decide the fate of slavery in these territories, this act also set the stage for the beginning of the U.S. Civil War. After the passage of the act, pro-slavery and anti-slavery groups flooded the territory and infiltrated many tribal nations' boundaries with hopes of pushing their respective agendas within the new territory, through both political and violent means. The reservations of eastern Kansas became the battleground of a divisive civil conflict often called "Bleeding Kansas."[7]

In the same year that the Kansas-Nebraska Act passed, the official representatives of the Miami Nation journeyed to Washington, DC to negotiate a new treaty with the United States. In this treaty, the Miami Nation was forced to relinquish all but 70,000 acres of their lands. The treaty stated that within four months of completing a survey of the reservation, the nation would subdivide the remaining 70,000 acres into individual allotments of 200 acres each.

The treaty explicitly recognized any remaining lands as "the common property of the tribe," which would be used to provide for future generations.[8]

The United States sought this treaty in order to open up more of the arable lands of eastern Kansas to settlers. The Miami Nation, as well as other tribal nations, had reservations that spanned most of the river valleys and therefore the best farmland in the region. In the 1850s, some government officials believed that another removal was needed in order to completely free the land for settlement. Other officials pushed for diminishment of the larger reservations as a starting point. The Miami Nation chose to support diminishment in order to consolidate their holdings in a manner that would protect their property from theft and destruction from squatters, travelers heading west on the Santa Fe trail, and from their tribal neighbors. It was thought that an increased presence of Euro-American settlers with a long-term vested interest in the region would lead to more protections and a stable legal order.[9]

In 1857, under the terms of the aforementioned treaty, citizens of the Miami Nation selected 162 allotments of 200 acres each. This first round of allotments left the nation with 37,600 acres held in common for future generations. By 1869, this number was reduced to 10,000 through the creation of additional allotments. By accepting allotment of some of their land base, they believed that they would gain legal status similar to American settlers in Kansas Territory and benefit from the protections afforded individual land against squatters and theft of timber, cattle, and crops. By retaining "excess" acreage as land in common, the nation maintained a collective resource that could be used following patterns that were generations old before the first Treaty of Greenville in 1795.[10]

In 1861, at the start of the United States Civil War, Kansas became the 34th state, and after the completion of the Civil War, Euro-American migration to Kansas drastically increased. These new settlers saw all of the tribal nations in Kansas as a general impediment to progress. In 1864, the Miami Nation's Indian Agent G.A. Colton asserted that the "Indian lands are the best in the State, and justice would demand... that these fertile lands should be thrown open to settlement, and the abode of civilized and industrious men." Unwilling to wait for the lands to legally open for settlement, many settlers began to build houses, farm, and construct fences on the Miami Nation's undivided collective lands. These squatters were acting against the expressed wishes of the Miami Nation and in defiance of treaties and United States federal law. Federal and state officials often stood in opposition to the squatters, because their actions generated chaos and negatively impacted organized attempts to sell and tax Indian lands. Yet railroad companies, land speculators, squatters, and government officials were completely unified behind the goal of removing tribal nations from the state of Kansas. As in Indiana, this chaotic combination of interests put intense pressure on the Miami Nation to cede their lands and remove.[11]

In addition to the attempts to diminish the Miami Nation's homeland, a second and newer threat emerged. This threat was the result of United States officials' attempts to decrease the numbers of tribal nations by pushing smaller nations to merge together and cede their sovereignty to a larger tribal nation. In the late 1840s, the United States took this policy stance because they found managing multiple tribes with small populations difficult and inconvenient. They hoped that a smaller number of larger tribes would be easier to manage. To achieve this goal, the federal government tried to impose confederation – the legal combination of smaller tribes into one group with one governing body. In Kansas, the Miami Nation became a target of these efforts as they were pushed towards consolidating with the Wea, Piankashaw, Peoria and Kaskaskia, who had already agreed to confederate in 1832 and formalized that agreement by treaty in 1854.[12] A majority of the Miami Nation resisted these efforts, and as a result came into repeated conflict with the Peoria Chief, Baptiste Peoria, and the local Indian Agents, with whom he was working closely as an official government translator.[13]

In 1860, the Miami Nation publicly voiced their displeasure with Baptiste Peoria along two lines. First, they argued, "he does not conduct himself in such manner as an Officer should. For when we have business with our agent he is often in an unfit state caused by drunkenness." Second, they claimed, "if the business does not suit him or does not go as he wants it to he will break off and go to drinking and we are left without an interpreter just at such time as we want one most."[14] Accusations of drunkenness were commonly used to attack the character of individuals with whom one disagreed, and so those specific allegations were likely exaggerated. Far more serious and less prone to exaggeration were the accusations that Baptiste Peoria manipulated his role as interpreter to stop negotiations when they did not suit him. This accusation does not specifically reference confederation, but it is a clear sign that there were significant disagreements between Baptiste Peoria and the Miami National Council regarding leadership behavior and ethics.

This disagreement did not exemplify inter-tribal relations in this period. Instead, the Myaamia people often worked together with the other small tribes of Kansas and intermarried with many, including the Wea, Piankashaw, Peoria, and Kaskaskia. These alliances were always balanced with a strong focus on political and economic independence on the part of tribal leadership and tribal citizens.

Paralleling the failures to resist removal in Indiana, these attempts to weave a middle course through the tumultuous waters of the post-Civil War years in Kansas largely failed. American settlers refused to respect the individual land rights of Indians who were not citizens of the United States. Squatters permeated tribal lands and the theft of timber and animals was a constant source of harassment and a significant financial loss. In 1871, Miami leader Eecipoonkwia (John B. Roubidoux) estimated that there were between 300 and 400 squatters illegally living on the reservation and utilizing tribal resources. Eecipoonkwia publicly pleaded in the local newspapers, the LaCygne Journal and the Miami County Republican, "What rights have the settlers upon our lands? The answer is plain – none in justice or equity. But politically they have votes, and in this they are stronger than we. Our claims and rights are nothing."[15] Without access to the political system, the courts, or the support of federal agencies, the Miami Nation could not protect their shared common lands or their individual allotments. It is within this context that the United States government made the final push for the Miami Nation to relinquish all of its lands in Kansas and move for a second time.

A History of the Allotment of Miami Lands in Indian Territory

In 1867, the Miami Tribe negotiated their last treaty with the United States. In this treaty the nation agreed to relocate to the northeast corner of Indian Territory. The Confederated Peoria Tribe agreed that the Miami could purchase an undivided right to their reservation lands, which the Peoria purchased from the Quapaw and Seneca in the same treaty. The Miami also agreed to reconsider merging politically with the Confederated Peoria and were given two years within which to make their decision on this subject.

The terms of the 1867 treaty caused controversy within the Miami Nation. Six months after the signing of the treaty, the Miami Nation's assigned Indian Agent G.A. Colton wrote to the Commissioner of Indian Affairs, "There has been some little disturbance among the Miamis in consequence of misrepresentations circulated among them with reference to the contents of their treaty now pending before the United States senate." This "little disturbance" was, in part, caused by a faction of the Miami Nation that opposed removal to Indian Territory. The conflict led Miami leaders to communicate with government officials after the treaty about their concerns. As a result, the United States Senate struck out eleven articles of the 1867 treaty. The Senate did ratify Article XXVI, which described how the Miami Tribe could confederate with the Peoria, if they were willing, and how they could purchase land for a new reservation in Indian Territory (Oklahoma). However, the remainder of the terms of their removal to Indian Territory were left for a future negotiation to settle.[16]

At the time, there was a lot of confusion around the Miami position regarding the 1867 Treaty. In 1867, the yearly report of the Commissioner of Indian Affairs included a report on the Miami from Thomas Murphy, Superintendent of the Central Superintendency. One year after the treaty, Murphy observes, "These Indians [the Peoria], as well as the Miamies, have raised small crops of corn and nothing else, because they are in expectation of speedily removing to the Indian country south of Kansas, and appear to have lost all interest in the cultivation of their farms. Like most of the other tribes in Kansas they are exceedingly anxious to have their treaty ratified-which is now pending before the United States Senate-and remove to their new homes as speedily as possible."[17]

Murphy's 1868 report, only one year after the treaty, flipped the entire situation on its head. In it Murphy claimed, "The treaty made with the Miamies, and embraced in the above-named [1867] omnibus treaty, was, on account of innumerable contentions among themselves, not ratified by the Senate, but was referred back to the Indians and a new treaty ordered to be made. Since then, I am happy to state, they have compromised all their difficulties, and are now prepared to make such a treaty as they think will be satisfactory to themselves and acceptable to the honorable Senate of the United States."[18] Murphy did not list the points of contention, but there were three issues of common concern for Miami people in Kansas. First, since 1848, many Miami had expressed their desire to remain politically independent from the Confederated Peoria. Second, the Miami struggled to sell their unallotted land in Kansas because of problems with squatters. Many wanted to delay removal to Indian Territory until after they had received fair market value for their individual and communally held lands. Third, some individual Miami families wanted to remain in Kansas where they had only just begun to rebuild their lives and construct new homes and farms. On this last point, the U.S. was firm: the Miami Nation had to move to Indian Territory, and any individuals who stayed would sacrifice their tribal citizenship.[19]

The 1868 agreement that Murphy mentioned was never ratified. It may have been in the Senate's queue when, in 1871, an argument between the Senate and the House of Representatives led to the end of the entire system of American Indian-United States treaty-making.[20] After 1871, all new agreements between the United States and Tribal governments were handled through the legislative process and involved both houses of Congress. In 1871, no tribe possessed the legal wherewithal to mount a substantial challenge to this massive change in federal policy, and so treaty-making died without much legal protest. As with other events in our past, the Miami Nation was forced to navigate through these new currents and work with legislators in both houses of Congress in order to advance the interests of their nation.

In 1872, a contract was drawn up in which some citizens of the Miami

A History of the Allotment of Miami Lands in Indian Territory

Nation agreed to politically confederate with the Confederated Peoria. The contract was created after the expiration of the two-year window for confederation established by the Treaty of 1867, and evidence suggests that the portions referring to a political merger were never implemented. Throughout their last years in Kansas, the Miami Nation continued to administer its shared and collective lands and continued to meet and conduct itself as a sovereign tribal government.

The terms by which the Miami Nation moved to Indian Territory appear to have been settled by legislation passed on March 3, 1873. This legislation ordered the Secretary of the Interior to review a contract drawn up by the Miami Nation and the Confederated Peoria "and to approve the same with such modifications as justice and equity may require." After approving the contract, the Secretary "may withdraw from said consolidated fund, and pay to the confederated Wea, Peoria, Kaskaskia, and Piankeshaw Indians... for an interest in the lands of the last-named confederated tribe, for all of said Miamis, electing as aforesaid, to unite with said confederated tribe." According to the legislation, after the union of the Miami Nation with the Confederated Peoria was completed, "the united tribe shall be called the United Peorias and Miamis."[21]

All of the currently available evidence indicates that the Miami Nation decided not to politically consolidate with the Confederated Peoria. The evidence clearly demonstrates that the Miami Nation maintained a separate and uninterrupted tribal government from 1867 in Kansas, through the years in Indian Territory (1873-1907), and into the contemporary statehood era in Oklahoma (1907-present). Shortly after the 1873 legislation, Ely Geboe explained the Miami Nation's understanding of consolidation in a letter to the Quapaw Agency Superintendent Hiram W. Jones:

> Our people are all agreed to continue their Chiefs Tho. Miller Head Chief and David Geboe Second Chief, and they have also appointed Two Councilmen, John Lum Ke Com Wah and Peter La Falier for the term of good behavior. And also our people have empowered us to sign any papers for them in their behalf. and [sic] our people wish to continue their Chiefs

after the consolidation with the Peorias and to hold the same privilege as the Peorias, as our Bill does not make any distinction. But the two tribes shall be called the United Peorias and Miamies.[22]

In this letter, Geboe communicated his nation's intent to continue with their own form of government after joining the Peoria on their shared reservation in Indian Territory. The behavior of tribal government and its citizens as preserved in the documentary record of the nation and within community memory reflects this steadfast desire to maintain the integrity of the Miami Nation. In contrast, legislators in Washington, DC, who were distant from Indian Territory and uninterested in the intricacies of native nations, remained mostly oblivious to this important political distinction and much of the language in legislation passed from 1867-1889 is reflective of this lack of on-the-ground knowledge.

The chaos caused by the differing perceptions among legislators, agency officials, and tribal governments endured until 1899, when the Federal Government acknowledged that they had been interacting with the Miami Nation as a separate tribal government. In that year, the Acting Commissioner of Indian Affairs A.C. Tanner wrote to Miami Nation Chief Thomas Richardville to explain his Department's perception of this chaotic period. Tanner began by stating that the "act of March 3, 1873, provided for the union of the Confederated, Peoria &c, Indians with the Western Miami Indians." Tanner went on to acknowledge that "Although this act seemed to unite the several tribes into one, this office appears to have dealt with the Western Miamis separately from the Confederated, Peorias, &c." Tanner then referred to the March 2, 1889 allotment act, which specifically delineates two separate tribes "the Confederated, Wea &c. tribe of Indians, and the Western Miami tribe of Indians." The Commissioner concluded by clarifying that, "Whatever may have been the situation before the passage of this act, it seems to be clear that the Western Miamis have since that date at least been recognized as a separate tribe." As further evidence of the political separation, Tanner pointed out, "Congress has also made the Peorias citizens of the United States, while such action has not been taken so far as the Miamis are concerned."[23]

A History of the Allotment of Miami Lands in Indian Territory

In his 1899 letter, Tanner failed to acknowledge that the Miami Nation continued to hold elections for tribal offices and met regularly as the Miami National Council throughout the period of time in which he feels their status was ambiguous from the perspective of the Department of the Interior and Congress. Despite this bureaucratic uncertainty, election results and countless Miami National Council minutes were included in the volumes of correspondence between the Miami Nation and the Department of the Interior stretching back into the 1860s.

The sum total of this evidence makes it clear that the Miami Nation maintained governmental and community integrity during the difficult period of transition from Kansas to Indian Territory. Our communal craft was besieged with waves on all sides, but the mihsooli held together, and the nation found their way through the danger. However, the story of this second forced removal remains more chaotic than the 1846 forced removal. A part of this chaos was the result of greater "freedom." The federal government left it up to the Miami to move themselves to their shared reservation in Indian Territory. Some Miami families began arriving as early as 1871 and some families made the move as late as 1884.[24] The majority of the first person accounts of this removal describe that most citizens of the Miami Nation moved directly to lands within their reservation. These families immediately began to build homesteads, put up fences, graze their animals, and plant crops.

The Land and the People in Indian Territory (1873-1890)

In 1937, Nannie Lee Burns - working under a Works Progress Administration grant - interviewed Mrs. Elizabeth 'Lizzie' Lindsey Palmer (Allottee biography on page 96). Lizzie was the daughter of Mary Pesawah, a Myaamia woman, and Marcus Lindsey, Peoria man. Following Marcus's death, Lizzie's mother married Thomas Richardville (Allottee biography on page 91). As a result, the young Lizzie spent a lot of time with Thomas as a child. As an adult, Lizzie was one of the many citizens of the Miami Nation forced to move to the shared Miami-Peoria Reservation in Indian Territory in the 1880s. Lizzie Palmer told Burns, "Chief Richardville had arranged and bought for the Miamis sufficient land from the Peorias for each of the tribe living in Kansas to have 200 acres each. The land laying west and south of the Quapaws and west of the Peorias."[25] Mrs. Palmer reported to Burns that "all of the Miamis did not come at one time but came a family or several families at a time over a period of several years and that all of them never came which resulted in a surplus of land." Palmer recalled that the Richardville family moved west of Commerce in 1882 and that she and her husband "came in the early spring of 1884" and went "directly to her land and her son's" land to the north of the eventual location of the town of Miami. Immediately upon arrival, Mr. Palmer began "ploughing and preparing to make a home."[26]

These efforts to settle and improve individual parcels are remarkable because they occurred eight years prior to the official allotment of the reservation in 1892. This indicates that the Miami Nation and the Confederated Peoria informally grouped themselves into tribal zones when settling the shared reservation. These tribal zones were further subdivided into family clusters. These settlement patterns also seem to anticipate the allotment of the reservation. It is also striking that the process of settling the reservation did not produce much conflict within or between the two tribes.

Because the Miami Nation made the move from Kansas to Indian Territory (see Figure 2 on page 45) as family units, it was natural for them to group themselves into clusters of individual tracts based largely on extended kin networks. The majority of these clusters lie to the northwest of what became the town of Miami, east of the Neosho River, and south of the Kansas border. These groupings are similar to what Lizzie Palmer described above. However, a few Myaamia families settled homesteads in lands to the north of the eventual Miami town site. In a similar but inverted pattern, citizens of the Confederated Peoria Tribe established homesteads largely to the north and east of the Miami town site running all the way to the Missouri border, with some Peoria sprinkled within and around the Miami clusters in the previously described areas. It is critical to note that some of these decisions regarding homestead placement occurred as early as twenty-one years before allotment tracts were surveyed and patented in 1890.

A History of the Allotment of Miami Lands in Indian Territory

The movement to officially allot the Miami and Peoria Reservation began in 1885 as the Miami National Council resolved to "petition to Congress" to pursue "an allotment Bill to allot our part of the Peoria and Miami lands amounting to 17,083 acres in severalty, each head to share, not to exceed 220 acres."[27] This bill did not make its way successfully through Congress. By November of 1886, the Miami National Council petitioned Congress to add amendments to the bill regarding patents in fee and other minor restrictions. If the House failed to amend the bill, the Council asked that the bill be pulled from the floor.[28] Whatever the circumstances, this House bill did not pass Congress.

Why were Miami people seeking so readily the allotment of their lands in Indian Territory? The answer to this question is unsurprisingly complicated. First, as early as 1879, tribes in Indian Territory heard rumors that American settlers were plotting to forcibly seize their lands. In response, the U.S. government issued proclamations stating that Indian lands in Indian Territory would soon be allotted, which would make squatting more difficult and potentially open up lands for purchase by those who wanted legal title to land in the Territory.[29] The Miami had extensive experience with squatters in Kansas and had learned the hard lesson that once their land was occupied it was nearly impossible to force the squatter out or even get fair market value for their land, if they wanted to sell it. In the face of outright theft, the division of collective reservation lands into individual parcels presented an opportunity to avoid losing all of their lands. After thirteen treaties and nearly 100 years of government-to-government relationship with the United States of America, Miami people realized they could easily end up with no land base if they did not act to protect it.

A second reason that the Miami Nation pursued allotment was that by asserting their sovereignty and making petitions for allotment together with the Peoria, they created an opportunity to manage allotment on their own terms as much as was possible. This strategy bore fruit as combined efforts of the Miami and Peoria Tribes eventually led to a bill that granted 200 acres to each individual, which was higher than the 160 acres the Dawes Act promised to tribes located outside of Indian Territory (Oklahoma). Initially, they set their sights even higher with a proposed upper limit of 220 acres, but this quantity was rejected by the legislature.[30]

In 1887, the General Allotment Act, also known as the Dawes Act, was signed into law. However, it contained exemptions for most of the tribes of Indian Territory including the Miami Nation. The exemption for Indian Territory tribes was partly the result of the lobbying efforts of the Cherokee, Choctaw, Chickasaw, Creek, and Seminole. The leaders of these larger tribes perceived the General Allotment Act to be a threat to the leaders' control of their collective lands. The exemption was also the result of the separate lobbying efforts of American ranchers, who argued that individual property rights once granted to Indians would interfere with their established quasi-legal grazing practices.[31] It took two more years of work to have a separate allotment act passed on the Miami Nation's own terms.

From 1873 to 1890, the Miami Nation and the Confederated Peoria lived together on a shared reservation divided informally among family groups, many of whom built houses, improved the land around their homes, and began to farm and herd animals. Tribal members tended to group themselves together along family and tribal lines, and this resulted in a recognized Miami zone and a Peoria zone within the shared reservation. Each of these zones had a minor degree of overlap but for the most part each zone was perceived as belonging to the Miami Nation or the Confederated Peoria Tribe. The Miami often referred to their area as the "Miami Reservation." This terminology is used in the minutes of numerous Miami National Council Meetings and in many of the letters that the Council and its representatives signed.[32]

When the Miami National Council discussed issues pertaining to the legal administration of their common land base, they usually referred to the land directly as the "Peoria and Miami Reservation" and referenced the need for the two tribes to work together. For example, in September of 1887, the Miami Council discussed the need to confer with the Peoria Tribal government in order to pass legal codes regarding "descent, marriage, divorce, and roads." The pattern of behavior seems to have been that the Miami National Council perceived a space within the shared reservation as heavily Miami and they called this space the "Miami Reservation." But when it came to passing laws and officially allotting the shared land base, they recognized that it was a joint legal effort and required collaboration between the Miami National Council and the Confederated Peoria.[33]

By 1888, the Miami Nation and the Confederated Peoria united again in an effort to have their shared reservation allotted. Together, they sought a bill that would allot the shared reservation with 200 acres going to each member of each tribe regardless of age, gender, or marital status. This was a significant difference from the Dawes Act that provided for 160 acres to a head of household, 80 acres for unmarried individuals, and 40 acres for minors. If the Dawes Act or similar legislation had been applied to the Peoria and Miami Reservation, this would have resulted in a drastic increase in surplus lands. Surplus lands often fell victim to squatters and then could only be sold for far less than fair market value. By receiving allotments of 200 acres for all regardless of age or marital status, the Miami and the Peoria skillfully avoided having a large percentage of their reservation deemed surplus, and then lost to squatters or through a forced sale.

The Land and the People Divided:
The Allotment of the Miami Nation (1890-1905)

On March 2, 1889, an "Act to Provide for Allotment of Land in Severalty to United Peorias and Miamis in Indian Territory" was signed into law. The act provided that each citizen of the Miami Nation would receive "an allotment of land not to exceed two hundred acres." In addition, the act extended certain provisions of the Dawes Act (1887) to the "Confederated Wea, Peoria, Kaskaskia, and Piankeshaw tribes of Indians, and the Western Miami Tribe of Indians, now located in the northeastern part of the Indian Territory and to their reservation." The legislation specifically called out the maximum acreage to be allotted by each Tribe. This maximum acreage was proportional and based on how much land the Miami Nation purchased from the Peoria in 1873. The act states that Miami Nation acreage shall not exceed "seventeen thousand and eighty-three acres of said reservation," and no "more than thirty-three thousand two hundred and eighteen acres in the aggregate to the United Peoria Indians." These allotments would "not be subject to alienation for twenty five years from the date of the issuance of patent" and were protected from "levy, sale, taxation, or forfeiture for a like period of years."[34]

Upon the allotment of the Peoria and Miami Reservation, which reflected the above proportions, the shared administration of the land base should have come to an end. In simplest terms, once allotment was completed there was no reservation. The legislators who wrote the act tried to communicate their intent on this point by stating that once the aggregate acreage was allotted, "said amounts shall be treated in making said allotments in all respects as the extent of the reservation of each of said tribes, respectively." The goal of the legislation was to ensure that there would be no remaining land reserved for the common use of the Miami Nation and the Confederated Peoria Tribe. However, both nations saw their tribal populations shrink following the original removal treaty in 1867. The Miami Nation had many citizens who chose to remain in Kansas and some of those who removed to Indian Territory died of old age or disease before allotment could be completed. This left both nations proportionally with more land than people. As a result, allotment failed to completely eliminate the common lands of the Miami Nation and the shared Peoria and Miami reservation continued on in an extremely diminished form. The Miami owned an undivided right to 60% of the remaining reservation lands, but as with the original reservation, the administration of these lands continued to be shared with the Confederated Peoria.[35]

These remaining reservation lands, which the U.S. government referred to as "residue lands," were scattered throughout the entire shared area running from the Kansas border through to the Missouri border (see Figure 3 on page 46). Unlike the excess lands in Kansas, these unallotted acres were not as attractive for squatters. The theft of timber and illegal or unethical grazing leases remained a problem, but because of the scattered geography and small size of the parcels, it was unlikely that a squatter could easily build a homestead anywhere within the remaining reservation.

A History of the Allotment of Miami Lands in Indian Territory

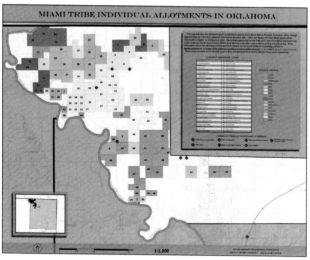

Miami Tribe of Oklahoma allotment map by Bradford Kasberg, depicting all 66 Miami allotments, color coded to show family grouping. A larger version of this map can be found on page 46.

The 1889 legislation set out a procedure for selecting allotments that was slightly more liberal than the Dawes Act. The Peoria and Miami Act stated, "all allotments" were "to be selected by the Indians, heads of families selecting for their minor children, and the chiefs of their respective tribes for each orphan child." The Dawes Act gave the Indian Agent more influence in the selection process than the 1889 legislation.

As demonstrated by the stories of Elizabeth Palmer (Allottee biography on page 96) and her son Harley Palmer (Allottee biography on page 97), most tribal citizens settled on their future allotments when they arrived from Kansas. Most families grouped their allotments together in clusters. In Figure 3 on page 46, the family allotment clusters are noted by color. There were a few individual allotments that were isolated from those of the rest of their family, but these were often smaller "bottom forty" parcels which held valuable timber used for the construction of structures and fences on their new farms. It appears that the intent, at least at first, was to select lands that made it possible to group family farms together. This would have made it easier to draw on family assistance for the hard work of building and maintaining farms.

By April 1890, the vast majority of the Miami Tribe had completed the process of selecting, surveying, and patenting their allotments.[36] There are some references to members of the Drake and Bright families attempting to select additional 40-acre allotments as late as 1896, but no record has been found to demonstrate that these allotments were ever created. The speed of this process was probably accelerated by the fact that most families had preselected their land in anticipation of earlier allotment efforts. In this initial allotment process, there does not appear to have been any conflict between the Miami Nation and the Confederated Peoria Tribe. Additionally, there were only a few minor conflicts between citizens of the Miami Nation, and these were successfully resolved through internal tribal mediation.[37]

Beginning in 1892, two years after allotment concluded, the Miami Nation and the Peoria Tribe jointly lobbied for the allotment of their respective portions of the remaining common reservation lands. The Miami Nation specifically sought to allot these lands to those born after the 1890 allotment and, if possible, to provide additional land to those who already received their 200 acres. On March 5,1892, Thomas Richardville (Allottee biography on page 91) represented both the Miami Nation and the Peoria Tribe in testifying before a Congressional Hearing on allotment. In his testimony, Richardville described the areas that the Miami Nation and the Peoria Tribe identified as potentially being allotted to their respective citizens. He stated that the Miami would like the fractional parcels near the Kansas border and the Peoria Tribe members would like the parcels along the southern border of the Quapaw allotments. Four months later, Peoria Chief Frank Beaver arrived in Washington, DC to "assist my friend, Mr. Richardville, in disposing of our surplus lands."[38] Despite at least four months of lobbying and testimony, Congress did not act in any way on the desires of the Miami Nation.

Efforts to allot the remaining acreage apparently continued throughout the 1890s. In September of 1895, Thomas Richardville received a letter from the Commissioner of Indian Affairs D.M. Browning that stated, "the matter of allotting the Confederated Peorias, etc. and the Miamis has been closed. No further allotments can be made on these reservations under existing law."[39] Both tribes had enough experience with the inconsistent nature of federal Indian policy to pursue an amendment to the 1889 law that would allow them to request new allotment patents and also pursued the sale of this shared "excess" acreage. These joint Miami and Peoria requests continued through 1902, when Congress passed the desired amendment. This amendment repealed the 25-year restriction on the sale of surplus lands held in common by the Miami Nation and the Peoria Tribe. In 1903, these surplus lands were sold in an auction involving a sealed bidding process. The U.S. government refused to allot the surplus lands to Miami citizens and conflicts over squatters, illegal timbering, and unethical leasing caused conflict between the Miami Nation and the Peoria Tribe. By selling these lands, the leadership of the Miami Nation transformed the conflicted lands into a cash resource. However, the sale of these lands meant that the Miami Nation no longer held lands in common.[40]

During the original debates over allotment in the U.S. Senate, Senator Henry M. Teller predicted that "when thirty or forty years shall have passed and these Indians shall have parted with their title, they will curse the hand that was raised professedly in their defense to secure this kind of legislation."[41] Tragically, it came to pass much as he described, and the end of patent protections quickly spelled the end of tribal land ownership. As a result of the Miami Nation's allotment, what was once a shared common resource became separated from the Nation. By the 1920s, the Nation and many of its citizens were landless. After thirteen treaties and 125 years of government-to-government relationship with the United States, the Miami Nation had been completely divested of what was arguably its second most important resource: land.

The process by which the Miami Nation and many of its citizens became landless was more complex than the simple evil manipulations of a cursed "hand" rigging the system against the nation. The allotment process was designed to break communal groups into relatively independent nuclear families who would have the "freedom" to choose where to work, where to live, and how to dispose of their property, including land. This apparent "freedom to choose" produced worse outcomes for the nation than the Kansas squatters who stole the nation's lands through violent intimidation. Instead, allotment created an experience where tribal land loss appeared to be the product of the community's own choices. To those unfamiliar with tribal history, allotment made it appear that citizens of the Miami Nation intentionally chose to give up their communal lands.

The Land, the People, and the Miami Nation After Allotment (1905-1939)

Allotment was intended to be the last step of a long process to divest the Miami Nation of its shared land base. The beginnings of this process stretch back to the Miami Nation's first land treaty signed at Greenville, Ohio in 1795. For generations, common land allowed the Miami Nation to protect its future against the personal desires of any individual or group of individuals. In the 1800s, the Miami Nation's experience with war, treaties, forced removal, boarding schools, and the emerging American economic system created pressures that convinced Miami people that individual land ownership was the best way to ensure their family's health and stability. They came to believe that owning land in common was restricting economic and political freedom. Private land ownership and the "freedom" it supposedly brought were perceived by many to be the best path by which individuals and their families could be healthy, stable, and secure. In the end, many Miami families found this stability by selling their lands in Ottawa County and moving to other parts of Oklahoma, Colorado, California, Oregon, and beyond. But as families sold their allotment lands, or lost their lands due to debt, the Miami Nation began to unravel as many of its citizens were forced into what essentially became a third removal. This process began to divest the nation of a significant portion of its most valuable resource: its people. In the history of the Miami Nation, there is a strong correlation between the existence of a shared national land base and the health of the nation, and today among Myaamia people there is a collective belief that the vitality of the Miami Nation is tied to the ability of its citizens to physically gather on lands that they call their own. Allotment forced Myaamia people into making a choice between the health of one's immediate family and the endurance of the nation's land base. This "choice" had the veneer of freedom but was heavily constrained by external forces at the local, state, and federal levels, which were all hostile to the continued existence of tribes and tribal lands.

David Chang in his study of the impact of allotment on the Creek Nation summarizes this fundamental hostility at all levels of American society:

> From the point of view of a middle-class white reformer in the 1880s who was dedicated to the notion that America marched forward, what could Indian land tenure represent but a brake on the progress of the nation? For a working-class white agrarian, what could Indian farmers, landlords, and governments mean but impediments on the path to white American land ownership and white American democracy? For white reformers and agrarians alike, for America to be America, Indian lands had to be allotted.[42]

In the decades that followed allotment, the economic and social forces produced by World War I, the Great Depression, and urbanization created immensely powerful rapids that drove many citizens from the community mihsooli. One could argue that with the loss of shared lands, the community canoe began to break apart. This environment of disintegration is also what pushed the Miami language and significant elements of Miami culture into dormancy.

The first requests for the sale of Miami national lands in Indian Territory were connected to the unallotted parcels scattered throughout the formerly shared reservation mentioned above. But as the older allottees began to pass away, the nation requested that the original restrictions against sale be removed from inherited allotments. In 1900, the U.S. Congress approved a process by which heirs could sell their parents' and grandparents' lands following their death.[43] As result, the death of allottees often resulted in the original reservation lands leaving Myaamia possession. Heirs often sold the land to pay off their own or inherited debt, for economic gain, or simply because, if they were from a small family, they could not manage the increased acreage. This type of land loss made it difficult for the Miami Nation to provide for future generations. The system of land ownership fostered by allotment made it impossible for the nation to balance the needs of bigger and smaller families. Some Myaamia families had large numbers of children, who provided necessary labor for running a farm in the late nineteenth and early twentieth centuries, and after 100 years of population decline these large families helped stabilize and then increase the overall population of the Miami Nation. But as these children came of age, only one or two could inherit enough land to sustain their own family as an adult. As a result, many young Miami adults moved to other places to find work and sustain their own growing families.

As the oldest generation among the allottees aged, they struggled to work their land and often desired to sell in order to move to local towns for retirement. They also worried about the future of children and grandchildren who had been born after allotment and could gain no land from their tribal nations. In 1906, leaders from the Miami, Oklahoma area traveled to the town of Vinita in the Indian Territory to testify before the Select Senate Committee on Affairs in Indian Territory regarding the lifting of many of the restrictions on their peoples' allotments. No Miami leader attended this meeting, but the testimony of two Peoria men, John Wadsworth and George Finley, are good examples of feelings that many tribal people shared throughout the northeast corner of Indian Territory. John Wadsworth was 64 years old at the time of his testimony. Wadsworth was married to Sarah Wadsworth, who was Waayaahtanwa (Wea). In response to the Senate Committee's question regarding why he wanted the restrictions lifted on his allotment, Wadsworth replied, "Well, I have only a wife and myself. The children are all gone. I have 100 acres, and I want to sell it and go to town, for I am tired of farming, so I want to sell my land and go to town." At the end of his testimony he reiterated, "I want to get away from the farm. I am tired of it, and I want to go to town." The Wadsworth's experience was not unique, and many of their Myaamia relatives and neighbors suffered from the same exhaustion. Children and grandchildren born after allotment could receive no lands, and so they often left the area to seek work. As a result, aging parents had no help to run their labor-intensive farms, and therefore sought to fund their retirement in town by selling their lands.

George Finley also testified before the Senate Committee that day, but his reasons for seeking a lifting of restrictions were a little different from John

A History of the Allotment of Miami Lands in Indian Territory

Wadsworth. Finley, a Peeyankihšia (Piankashaw) by birth and a citizen of the Peoria through confederation, wanted to provide for his son, who was born after allotment. Finley explained his family's needs as follows:

> I want to say that we all want these restrictions removed. I have a personal reason for wanting these restrictions removed. I have two children, and one of them drawed [sic] an allotment and one of them didn't. The last child, the one that didn't draw an allotment, is crippled and never can work on a farm for he couldn't do anything, and I would like to have this allotment of mine in such shape that if I would lie down and die I could leave to the crippled child, for he needs it, and the other child don't as it has already an allotment. One of them is a girl and the other is a boy, and the girl has an allotment and the boy hasn't, so he needs what I have more than the girl does. I want it fixed so I can divide it between the wife and the boy.

Finley believed that the restrictions were hurting his family by limiting how he could pass his land on to his children. Finley perceived injustice in forcing allottees to divide their allotments among their children. Divided ownership limited the economic potential of the lands. Specifically, Finley worried that the restrictions would leave his disabled son at a further disadvantage in life. Finley and Wadsworth's weariness and frustration echo painfully throughout all of the testimony taken down that fall day in Vinita. While the lifting of restrictions sped the process of land loss for both the Miami Nation and the Peoria Nation, one can hardly judge John Wadsworth or George Finley for seeking to take care of themselves and their families.[44]

In 1909, Congress responded to the requests of men like George Finley and John Wadsworth by passing an "Act authorizing removal of restrictions upon lands of adult allottees except a tract of not less than 40 acres." This one legislative act made it possible for 80 percent of Myaamia lands to be sold prior to the expiration of the twenty-five year protections originally promised under the 1889 Allotment Act.[45]

The land sale records in the Ottawa County courthouse demonstrate the sale of Myaamia allotments accelerated in the early 1900s and reached a critical mass in 1915 with the expiration of the original twenty-five year protections from sale, taxation, or seizure. The reasons for selling land aligned fairly closely to John Wadsworth's statement. Most young Myaamia people had moved away from the former reservations, and their parents were exhausted from a lifetime of hard labor on their farms. Additionally, the economic downturns that followed the end of World War I forced many families to sell their land. In some cases, the banks seized former allotments, allotment homes, and all movable property, as families could no longer make good on their debts.

The struggle to maintain allotment lands following the lifting of restrictions is well illustrated by the story of the Drake family and the lands of Siipiihkwa, also known as Jane Pigeon Drake (Allottee #16 on page 67). Siipiihkwa was born in 1846, the year of the Tribe's first forced removal from Indiana. She grew up in Indiana and as a young child moved to Kansas Territory. As a young adult in Kansas she married a non-Myaamia man, Milton Drake Sr. Siipiihkwa and Milton had fourteen children together, eleven of whom survived into adulthood. In the 1870s the couple moved their family to Indian Territory onto the Peoria and Miami Reservation. The couple built a large farm on the lands that would become Siipiihkwa's allotment and later expanded by purchasing nearby lands. By the early twentieth century, according to her grandson, Siipiihkwa's farm operations consisted of "2200 acres of grass, farm, and 900 acres of bottom land – 500 ton hay barn – huge granaries, corrals and hog-tight fenced acres for cattle and hogs."[46] At the time of Milton Sr.'s death in 1905, Siipiihkwa was over sixty years old and in ill health, and she struggled to manage the farm. For a few years after Milton's death, Siipiihkwa rented the farm and its operations to a local family. This family had run the farm nearly completely into the ground. Siipiihkwa's grandson recalled that the farm "was a disgrace." The family house "was so dirty it stunk" with "baby droppings all over the house and worse in the yard." The renters, Teddy remembered, had not used the outhouse, and "everything had been sold, stolen, or rotted out." There were no remaining "livestock, hogs, or poultry" and the "weeds were ten feet high around [the] barns and in [the] corrals and hog pens." The renters had not planted anything for years, and as a result the fields were covered in weeds, and the fence lines were in total disrepair.[47] In response to the chaos on Siipiihkwa's farm, the family convinced one of her and Milton's sons, John Logan Drake (Allottee #23 on page 74), to return home and take over the operation of the family farm.

During his childhood, John Drake worked on his parents' farm but as a young adult he traveled far and wide for work. In addition to owning a saloon in Hattonville (Commerce, Oklahoma), John also worked for the O'Hagan and Lake Railroad constructing right-of-ways. John married a Myaamia woman, Della Mary Leonard. Della was the daughter of an allottee but was too young to have received an allotment herself. John and Della traveled to the west of Oklahoma while he worked as a "foreman for excavation and tunnels and grades" on western railroads. Prior to the birth of their first child in 1910, John and Della returned to the Spavinaw Hills in Oklahoma to live near John's brother Milton (Allottee #22 on page 73).[48]

Descendants, and their spouses, of allottee Siipiihkwa (Jane Drake) gather for the dedication of the Drake House, 2006.

After their first child died in infancy, John returned to working for the O'Hagan and Lake Railroad, and he and Della moved to a new work site in Paducah, Kentucky. In 1911, prior to the birth of their second child, they returned to Oklahoma to lands near the Kansas border, on which John's brother Wayne (Allottee #12 on page 63) had a small homestead. In addition to the small summer farm and house, Wayne owned a general store in Edna, Kansas. While living with his brother Wayne, John made his first investments in cattle and land in the Spavinaw Hills, about 40 miles south of the Miami Nation's allotted lands near where Spavinaw Creek meets the Neosho River. John and three of his brothers built a series of small structures on these lands with the hopes of being "eligible for leasing government grazing land for cattle in Spavinaw Hills." Eventually they leased around 4,000 acres of government land in the Spavinaw Hills.

In the immediate aftermath of allotment, the Drake family story appears to be one of relative financial success. But this success proved to be fleeting. In the decade or so following the expiration of legal protections for Miami allotments, most Miami lands were sold or seized by banks for outstanding debt, and this was equally true of the Drake family farm. Decades later, Siipiihkwa's grandson summed it up with the simple but pained aside: "all good things come to an end."[49]

In the initial years following the return to Siipiihkwa's farm, John and Della's family remained prosperous. They absorbed the costs of new construction and livestock purchases without too much burden. Another sign of available cash and credit, John Drake also continued to make additional investments outside of the family farm. For example, John and Della were partners "in [a] big saw mill in [the] river bottom" where they "made ties for railroads and mine shaft shoring timbers for lead and zinc mines," from Picher, OK to Joplin, MO where there were "many, many big mining companies."[50]

However, the financial success that facilitated the Drake family's investments in cattle and timber came crashing down around the family following the collapse of farming commodity prices at the end of World War I. John's son, Teddy Drake, recalled, "Dad borrowed enough money from the Bank of his good friend Roy Wills in Miami to buy five hundred head of the 'white-faced' Herefords – [he was] gonna start a new breed of meat cattle." When "World War I stopped and the price of beef fell out of sight; Dad sold the cattle he had managed [on] the Place for $75.00 a head, less than he paid for them after feeding them all winter – all the calves went, too – for free." The economic downturn affected more than the price of beef, and the collapse of prices for agricultural goods put the family in a position where they could no longer pay their debts. Teddy Drake painfully recalled, "Finally the day arrived [when] the Bank foreclosed – [they] attached all properties of John L. and Della M. Drake – everything but our clothes and blankets for warmth." The family's property was sold in a "public sale at [the] Miami Fair Grounds," and the family moved to Commerce. John "had rented a furnished house there." Teddy Drake concluded, "[the] bank took everything but our clothes."[51]

As the story of John and Della Drake demonstrates, the ending of restrictive protections of the allotments of Miami Nation accelerated the loss of former reservation lands. Some Myaamia people viewed the ending of the restrictions as a positive step, which removed the often-oppressive oversight and control enforced by a government-appointed Indian Agent. But the end of restrictions also created a new environment whereby individual decisions, bad luck, and international economic forces could lead towards a future where the nation was landless and its citizens no longer lived within a consolidated area. A few steadfast families, like the Geboe and the Miller families, maintained their allotments through this period of heavy loss. Yet, the overall pattern was still one of loss and population out-migration. By the end of the 1920s, the Miami Nation was landless and most of its citizens did not own land within its former reservation. Instead, they had begun to scatter all over the country in search of jobs and new homes distant from their tribal nation.

Eventually community members began to recognize what was happening. A few knowledgeable elders within the community stated that some citizens feared that the nation might completely disintegrate and come to an end. Despite the fear and incredible sense of loss, these elders and many others maintained hope and continued the struggle for collective survival. As a result of their struggles, the Miami Nation endured.

The terrible economic times of the Great Depression created many challenges, but they also created a key change in the surface currents of federal Indian policy. At the highest levels of the federal bureaucracy, the official policy shifted from tribal dissolution and assimilation to actively supporting tribal economic self-sufficiency and through economic redevelopment, supporting overall tribal redevelopment. The Indian Reorganization Act (1934) and its companion Oklahoma Indian Welfare Act (1936) created a means, limited though it was, for tribes to redevelop their economies. Many of the policies of this period were generally patronizing, patriarchal, and ethnocentric; however, some of the changes were motivated by an honest horror, on the part of the United States, at what the allotment era and the Great Depression had done to Indian Country. Most importantly, laws were passed that reaffirmed the legal legacy of treaties and recognized the inherent retained rights of tribal peoples to exist and to govern themselves.

The Oklahoma Indian Welfare Act, much like the Indian Reorganization Act, sought to address what Commissioner of Indian Affairs John Collier identified as the fatally flawed policies of allotment and assimilation.[52] The act authorized the Secretary of the Interior to take lands into trust on behalf of tribes. This mechanism created the legal means by which shared collective tribal lands could be reacquired, maintained, and protected. The trust process and the protections it provided still implied that tribal peoples could not take care of themselves, but it nevertheless created a means to exert tribal sovereignty within a collectively-held land base. In contrast to reformers of the 1800s, this set of legislative acts, dubbed the Indian New Deal, opened an important series of doors that made it possible for tribes to rebuild in ways that avoided many of the traps created in the middle to late 1800s.[53]

Uniting Land and Uniting People: The Enduring Miami Nation (1939-Today)

In the years that followed allotment, the loss of tribal land paralleled the decline of tribal coherence and a general weakening of the Miami Nation. In

A History of the Allotment of Miami Lands in Indian Territory

1939, citizens of the Miami Nation reorganized their tribal government under the terms laid out in the Oklahoma Indian Welfare Act (Thomas-Rogers Act).[54] Under this law, the Miami Nation reformed itself as the Miami Tribe of Oklahoma. In 1939, the Miami Tribe of Oklahoma ratified their first written constitution and restructured their elected tribal leadership into a "Business Committee" made up of a Chief, Second-Chief, Secretary-Treasurer, and two Councilmen. This elected body was to run the business of the nation and represent the will of the Miami Council – all tribal citizens of voting age (21) who participated directly in tribal government. One of the major objectives of the Business Committee was to rebuild the economy of the nation and reacquire as much as possible of the national land base that had been lost through allotment. Over the decades that followed, the return of tribal lands paralleled an increase in tribal coherence and an increase in the health and stability of the nation. This increase was gradual, but it began in no small part because of the will of the people to hold land in common again as a nation.[55]

From 1903 until the 1970s the Miami Nation did not hold any land in common.[56] The return of historic tribal reservation lands began with an important act of family generosity. In 1975, the Miller-Moore family decided to donate a portion of the allotment lands of Esther Miller Dagenett back to the Miami Nation. This four-acre parcel was the first piece of the former Miami reservation returned to the nation to be held in trust for community use. In 1978, an Indian Action Team project built a one-story brick structure for the Miami Tribe of Oklahoma on Esther Miller Dagenett's allotment. This structure was initially called the Longhouse and was used for Tribal Council meetings and a wide variety of other community gatherings. When the Miami language began to be taught within the community again after decades of dormancy, the Longhouse became the first center of this educational effort. In 2008, the Longhouse was fittingly renamed the "Ethel Miller Moore Cultural Education Center" after the matriarch of the family who gifted this land to their nation.

Members of the Miller and Moore families gather at the rededication of the Miami Tribal Longhouse, now the Ethel Miller Moore Cultural Education Center, 2003.

Additionally, in 1976, a 41-acre parcel of land adjacent to Interstate 44 was legally reclassified as an Indian Reservation by the state of Oklahoma. This new reservation became the home of the Inter-Tribal Council, which originally included the Miami Tribe of Oklahoma and seven other tribes. Each tribe was given approximately five acres of the designated space on what became known as "8 Tribes Trail." In the years that followed the establishment of a Miami presence on these lands, the Miami Tribe built offices and a facility for supporting an elder's food program. This building became known as the Miami Tribe's headquarters and served as the gathering place of the General Council of the Miami Tribe of Oklahoma from the early 1990s until the opening of the Myaamia Community Center in 2010 on Newman Road, which is on the north side of Miami, Oklahoma within the historic "Miami zone" of the shared Miami and Peoria Reservation. The building on 8 Tribes Trail continues to serve as an important center for economic development, governance, and historic preservation for Myaamia people and the Miami Nation, but the land upon which it sits is unique in that it is shared among all of the nine tribes who today form the Inter-Tribal Council.[57]

A History of the Allotment of Miami Lands in Indian Territory

Following the reorganization of the Miami Tribe of Oklahoma in 1939 and the reacquisition of a national land base beginning in the 1970s, the Tribe began to develop a small but stable economic base. The strengthening economy was focused on two main objectives: providing for the needs of tribal citizens, especially elders and children, and the continued rebuilding of a national land base. From the 1990s through 2015, the Miami Tribe of Oklahoma purchased parcels of the Isadore Labadie allotment, the Jane Drake allotment and home, the David Geboe allotment and home, the Elizabeth Valley allotment, the Harley Palmer allotment, and many other parcels adjacent to historical allotments within the original boundaries of the Miami Reservation.

By 2014, the Miami Nation collectively owned slightly less than 1,600 acres of former reservation lands. Of the overall 1,600 acres, 133 have been placed in trust with the United States government. It is on trust lands that the Miami Nation can best exert their sovereign status through tribal law and tribal economic development.[58] Currently, most tribal activities – governmental, educational, or service-oriented – take place on land held by the Miami Nation. This rapid and surprising return of collectively held land has been paralleled by a similar increase in citizens participating in the life of the nation.

In addition to reacquiring the parts of the shared reservation allotted to Miami Nation citizens, the nation continues to seek the return of unallotted parts of the reservation to tribal control. Most of the unallotted lands were sold in 1903 and their unallotted status makes returning them to trust status extremely difficult. This process changed in 2014, when the Miami Tribe of Oklahoma and the Peoria Tribe of Oklahoma signed an agreement that each nation had the right to purchase former unallotted lands and put them into trust for the benefit of their nation. This agreement represents a continuation of over one hundred and forty years of sharing a reservation, living as close neighbors, and helping each other when needed.

In 2014, the Miami Tribe dedicated the akima kitahsaakana awiiki (Chief David Geboe allotment home) as an Historic Tribal Property. Purchased from Tribal citizen and David Geboe descendant Peggy McCord and her husband Bill, the home had remained in the Geboe family for five generations before returning to the Tribe as a community gathering place.

Part I Epilogue: The People Belong to The Land

The story of the allotment of the Miami Nation in Indian Territory is filled with challenge and loss, and yet through all of these difficulties the nation maintained some measure of control over our shared mihsooli (canoe). We survived as a nation, in no small part, because we strove to find a way to fiercely paddle together. In 1871, the Myaamia leader, Eecipoonkwia (John B. Roubidoux) argued that the Miami Tribe's reservation lands "belonged to the nation." It is easy to see how a tribal nation, like the Miami Tribe of Oklahoma, benefits from having a land base for governmental integrity and economic development. Of at least equal value is the importance of collective land to the people who make up the nation. There is something emotionally powerful about knowing that your people and your nation have a firm place to call "home." It is on these collective lands that citizens of the Miami Nation can speak their language and practice their culture, secure in the knowledge that these are places where they belong as a group. The nation and its people survived without legal control of a collective space, but most citizens would agree that we are healthier and more stable with our own lands upon which we can harvest, hunt, gather to celebrate and mourn, vote, preserve our history, teach our language and culture, and do all the things necessary for maintaining our collective mihsooli. Today, it is possible to add a contemporary conclusion to Eecipoonkwia's quote. Today, the Miami Nation can proudly proclaim that "the land belongs to the nation" and over time the nation has learned that it is equally true that "the nation and its people belong to the land." Allotment affected the Miami Nation's understanding of this sense of belonging, but it did not completely sever the land from its people. We survived allotment and perhaps have a greater appreciation of the value of shared lands as a result. myaamionka! moošaki aapweeyankwi myaamionkiši! - Miamis! We always return to Miami country!

Notes

1. This count does not include the 1828 treaty signed with the Thorntown village of Miami as the Miami Nation disputed its legitimacy at the time, or the treaties of 1832 and 1868/69, which were signed but never ratified.

2. GIS mapping estimates the section ceded in 1840 at 796,746 acres, the western section at 267,000 and the northern section at 209,000 acres. Leiter estimates that the Reserve contained 760,000 acres. Carl Leiter, "The Big Miami Reserve," Howard County Memory Project, http://www.howardcountymemory.net/default. aspx?id=12840, accessed April 29, 2015. Rafert reports that the western portion of the Reserve, ceded in 1834, was estimated to contain 208,000 acres. neewe (thank you) to Cameron Shriver for providing this GIS data. The remainder was ceded in 1840 and was estimated to contain 500,000 acres. Stewart Rafert, *The Miami Indians of Indiana: A Persistent People, 1654-1994* (Indianapolis, Ind.: Indiana Historical Society, 1996), 95-96, 99. John Tipton, *The John Tipton Papers, Vol. I*, eds. Nellie Armstrong Robertson and Dorothy Riker (Indianapolis: Indiana Historical Bureau, 1942), 42-43, 47-48.

3. Bert Anson, *The Miami Indians*, 1st ed. (Norman: University of Oklahoma Press, 1970), 239, 241 note 9.

4. For numbers and legal status see Kate A. Berry and Melissa A. Rinehart, "A Legacy of Forced Migration: the Removal of the Miami Tribe in 1846," *International Journal of Population Geography*, vol. 9 (2003), 102. Thank you to James Buss for providing a copy of Sinclair's letter, see List of Miamis Emigrated from Peru, In., October

14, 1846, National Archives and Records Administration, Microcopy 574, Special Files of the Office of Indian Affairs, 1807-1904. Roll 19, File 112. The text of the 1854 Treaty of Washington makes it clear that both the U.S. government and Miami people perceived the Miami Nation as centered in Kansas Territory while individual Miami families were residents of the state of Indiana. United States. 1904. *Kappler's Indian Affairs: Laws and Treaties, Vol II* (Washington, DC: U.S. Dept. of the Interior), 641-46. In the council that preceded the treaty, Mihšiinkweemiša stated "they have no power in [Indiana]—that power is in the tribe [in the] west, whatever that tribe does here will be binding upon the [Indiana] Miamies." neewe (thank you) to Cameron Shriver for sharing this document: 1854-55. MS Documents Relating to the Negotiation of Ratified and Unratified Treaties With Various Indian Tribes, 1801-1869. National Archives (United States). Ratified Treaty no. 274. Documents relating to the Negotiation of the Treaty of June 5, 1854, with the Miami Indians.

5. For a more complete story of the history of the Miami Nation in Kansas see Clarence E. Hayward, *The Lost Years: Miami Indians in Kansas* (Kansas City: Clarence Hayward, 2010) and Amy Bergseth, *"Our Claims and Rights are Nothing": Causes of Myaamia (Miami Indian) Removal from Kansas to Oklahoma"* (MA Thesis, University of Oklahoma, 2011).

6. Hayward, *Lost Years*, 17-38.

7. John Bowes, *Exiles and Pioneers: Eastern Indians in the Trans-Mississippi West* (New York: Cambridge University Press, 2007), 185-94; Bergseth, *"Our Claims and Rights are Nothing,"* 22-30.

8. Treaty of Washington, 1854 - United States. 1904. *Kappler's Indian Affairs: Laws and Treaties. Vol II*. Washington, DC: U.S. Dept. of the Interior, 641-46.

9. Bergseth, *"Our Claims and Rights are Nothing,"* 8-16.

10. Miami Reserve Matters - Statement of John Roubideaux, Head Chief of the Miami Indians in Kansas, Paola, Kansas, (1781), p.1. Roubidoux describes the remaining land as "held as the common property of the tribe." He does not specifically describe uses for this land, other than potential sale, but other sources indicate that the Miami were hunting and fishing throughout these lands.

11. Bergseth, *"Our Claims and Rights are Nothing,"* 45-56. W.M. Albin, Superintendent of the Central Superintendency, Annual Report on Indian Affairs, October 1, 1864, 391-92 (http://digital.library.wisc.edu/1711.dl/History.AnnRep64 accessed on March 23, 2017). For more on how opposing groups of Euro-Americans unified around the goal of forced removal see James Joseph Buss, *Winning the West with Words: Language and Conquest in the Lower Great Lakes* (Norman: University of Oklahoma Press, 2011), 60-64.

12. Anson, *Miami Indians*, 237-38. The Treaty of Washington 1854 recognized the union of the Wea, Piankashaw, Peoria and Kaskaskia, which was initiated in 1832. United States. 1904. *Kappler's Indian Affairs: Laws and Treaties. Vol II.* Washington, DC: U.S. Dept. of the Interior, 636-39.

13. Anson, *Miami Indians*, 237-38.

14. Minutes of the Miami National Council from November 12, 1860, Miami Nation Council Book 1, Myaamia Heritage Museum & Archive, Miami Tribe of Oklahoma, Miami, OK.

15. Miami Reserve Matters - Statement of John Roubideaux, Head Chief of the Miami Indians in Kansas, Paola, Kansas, (1781), 3.

16. Records of the Senate, the Senate struck Articles XXIX through XXXIX. 1867 Treaty United States. 1904. *Kappler's Indian Affairs: Laws and Treaties. Vol II.* Washington, DC: U.S. Dept. of the Interior, 960-67.

17. Thomas Murphy, Superintendent of the Central Superintendency, Annual Report on Indian Affairs, by the Acting Commissioner, November 15, 1867, 291-92. This annual report and all following reports from the Commissioner of Indian Affairs were accessed through Proquest Congressional.

18. Annual Report on Indian Affairs, November 23, 1868, 256-59.

19. These conclusions are based on the language in the 1873 legislation as well as the history of the Miami Nation following removal. March 3, 1873. I 17 Stat., 631., United States. 1904. *Kappler's Indian Affairs: Laws and Treaties, Vol. I* (Washington, DC: U.S. Dept. of the Interior), 145-48.

20. David E. Wilkins, American Indian Politics and the American Political System (Lanham, MD: Rowman & Littlefield), 110; Loring Benson Priest, *Uncle Sam's Stepchildren: The Reformation of United States Indian Policy, 1865-1887* (New Brunswick, Rutgers University Press,1942), 97-99; Francis Paul Prucha, *American Indian Treaties: The History of a Political Anomaly* (Berkeley: University of California Press, 1994), 289-310; Kevin Bruyneel, *The Third Space of Sovereignty: The Postcolonial Politics of U.S.-Indigenous Relations* (Minneapolis: University of Minnesota Press, 2007), 65-95.

21. *Kappler's Indian Affairs, Vol. I*, 148.

22. Ely Geboe et al, Neosho River, to Quapaw Agent Hiram W. Jones, November 22, 1874, Miami Papers Quapaw Agency Collection.

23. A.C. Tanner to Thomas Richardville dated May 31, 1899 (3826.2300 and 3826.2300.1), Thomas F. Richardville Collection, Gilcrease Museum, University of Tulsa.

24. Annual Report on Indian Affairs, November, 1871, 462. Elizabeth Lindsey Palmer, interview by Nannie Lee Burns, Indian-Pioneer Collection, Vol. 69, 0000, (1937), Western History Collections, University of Oklahoma, Norman, Oklahoma.

25. "Elizabeth Lindsey Palmer Interview," *Indian Pioneer Papers*, 3. Thomas Richardville reported to a Congressional hearing on allotment in 1892 that the Miami Nation paid the Peoria Tribe $1.50 an acre and that the payment was processed by the federal government. Hearing on Allotment of Lands in Severalty to Certain Indian Tribes, 39-40. William Nicholson to Hiram W. Jones, Receipt for payment for lands sold to the Miamis of Kansas, May 8, 1873, Quapaw Agency Records.

26. "Elizabeth Lindsey Palmer Interview," *Indian Pioneer Papers*, 3-4. In 1870 Enoch Hoag reported that all Osage Agency Indians (Kansas) had moved to Quapaw Agency in Indian Territory except the Miami. See Annual Report on Indian Affairs (October 31, 1870), 257. In 1871, only a few Miamis are reported to have moved to Indian Territory. See Annual Report on Indian Affairs, (November 15, 1871), 462, 499-500.

27. Miami Nation Council, Feb. 17th, 1885, Miami Nation Council Book 2, Miami Nation Council Book 1, Myaamia Heritage Museum & Archive, Miami Tribe of Oklahoma, Miami, OK, 11.

28. Peoria & Miami Reservation, Nov. 23rd, 1886, Miami National Council, Miami National Council Book 2, Miami Tribe of Oklahoma, Myaamia Heritage Museum and Archive, Miami, Oklahoma.

29. In April 1879, the Commissioner of Indian Affairs notified President Hayes that U.S. citizens, presumably in Kansas and Missouri, were planning to seize Indian lands in Indian Territory. See Wilcomb E. Washburn, *The Assault on Indian Tribalism: The General Allotment Act (Dawes Act) of 1887*, Harold M. Hyman ed. (Philadelphia: J.B. Lippincott Co., 1975), 6.

30. The Quapaws did the best of the Ottawa County tribes by increasing the limit to 240 acres per person. The Ottawa, for example, demonstrate how small allotments could be as each citizen was allotted only 80 acres. David Baird, *The Quapaw Indians: A History of the Downstream People* (Norman: University of Oklahoma Press, 1980), 139-42.

31. For more on the influence of cattlemen see Otis, *The Dawes Act*, 43; and Baird, *Quapaw Indians*, 127-28.

32. "Miami Reservation" shows up in the following minutes and letters in the Miami National Council Book 2: September 27, 1886,19; September 5, 1887, 24; September 7, 1887, 24; December 10, 1887, 35; December 18, 1888, 24 all in the Miami National Council Book collection Myaamia Heritage Museum and Archive; and in

the following miscellaneous Thomas Richardville letters: Report on an Election dated Jan 18, 1889; Letter from Commissioner of Indian Affairs to Agent Summers on April 5, 1887, all in the collection of the Myaamia Center. The 1890 House Report (51st Congress 1st Session House of Rep Report No. 1901) reads as follows "The real estate of these Indians [Miami Nation] was at one time held in common with the United Peorias, who also live in the Indian Territory. The estimated share of the Miamies is 17,083 acres."

33. For example, "Miami and Peoria Reservation" or "Peoria and Miami Reservation" are used in the following council minutes in the Miami National Council Book 2, September 27, 1886, 19; November 23, 1886, 20.

34. Stat. XXV., 1013 50th Congress Sess. II 1889 Chap. 422, see *Kappler's Indian Affairs, Vol. I*, 344-46.

35. Elizabeth Palmer Interview, Indian-Pioneer Collection, 3-4; Meghan Dorey's research on the "Western Miami Indian List" demonstrates that of the 85 Miami on the list in 1873, 33 died and 20 did not allot with the Miami Nation for other reasons. Natural population increase made up some of the losses, but in the end fewer came to Indian Territory than the nation had expected. As a result, there was a surplus of land.

36. April 15,1889 the Quapaw Agent Summers reported on Miami allotment acres as though the process was already completed. See Report of Secretary of Interior for 1889, 1863-64. There was one documented allotment in 1892 made to Edward Gibson Harris, a grandson of Eecipoonkwia (John B. Roubidoux).

37. The conflict over the inheritance of Rose Ann Sharkey's land and improvements occurred prior to the official allotment act and demonstrates that the nation was able to solve the problem internally before the official allotment and patenting of the land in 1890. Minutes of Miami National Council, on September 27, 1886, 17 and September 26, 1892, 33; in Miami National Council Book 2, Myaamia Heritage Museum and Archive.

38. In 1892, Thomas Richardville and Peoria Chief Frank Beaver jointly lobbied for the disposal of their unallotted lands. Thomas Richardville testified before the Senate Committee on Indian Affairs regarding "Allotment of Lands in Severalty to Certain Indian Tribes" on March 5, 1892, 39-50. Frank Beaver testified before the same body on July 9, 1892, 58-83.

39. D.W. Browning to Thomas Richardville, September 19, 1895, #3826.2297 in the Thomas F. Richardville Collection, Gilcrease Museum, University of Tulsa.

40. This amendment required that any debts owed to delegates or officers of the Miami Nation be paid first before any proceeds from the Miami sales went to

tribal citizens. 32 Stat., 245., May 27, 1902, in Kappler, Chapter 888 May 27, 1902.l 32 Stat., 245., 752. Deed of sale United States Government to George E. Nicholson, filed 23 April 1903.

41. Teller's quote "curse the hand" comes from debates in 1881 see Otis, *The Dawes Act*, 18.

42. David Chang, *The Color of the Land: Race, Nation, and the Politics of Land Ownership in Oklahoma, 1832-1929* (Chapel Hill: University of North Carolina Press, 2010), 71.

43. Miami Tribe to Congress, Sept 1, 1906 (#4027.8338, 4027.8338.1) and Miami Tribe to Congress, Dec 4, 1906, Thomas F. Richardville Collection, Gilcrease Museum, University of Tulsa. "SALE OF INHERITED LANDS, Miami and Peoria: (31 Stats. p. 248). Sec. 7, Provisions as to sale of inherited lands by heirs, -- hereby extended to heirs of allottees of Peoria and Miami Indians who were authorized by the Act of June 7, 1887, to sell a portion of their lands. Approved May 31, 1900".

44. Hearings of the Select Committee on Affairs in Indian Territory, U.S. Senate, Vinita, Indian Territory, November 13, 1906, 61-64.

45. "ACT OF CONGRESS. PUBLIC No. 306. H.R. 16743. An Act authorizing removal of restrictions upon lands of adult allottees except a tract of not less than 40 acres. Approved Mar. 3, 1909. (See Kappler on Indian Affairs, Vol. 1, Page 1040)."

46. Paul "Teddy" Drake, *An Autobiography by Teddy Drake (Written 1989-1990)*, ed. Daryll Williams (1992), Myaamia Heritage Museum and Archive (HC 1 Box 2 Folder 1), 9.

47. *An Autobiography by Teddy Drake*, 8.

48. *An Autobiography by Teddy Drake*, 3. John's wife Della Leonard Drake was the daughter of George Washington Leonard (Allottee #35).

49. *An Autobiography by Teddy Drake*, 4, 6.

50. *An Autobiography by Teddy Drake,* 3-7, 21, 31.

51. *An Autobiography by Teddy Drake*, 21, 31.

52. Scholars often paraphrase Collier as referring to allotment and assimilation as "twin evils." But he appears to have never used this phrase himself. The closest Collier comes to this phrasing was in a 1934 article in which he spoke of "the two fatal weaknesses of Indian administration" which were the "dissipation of the Indian estate and the progressive pauperization of the Indians" and "the suppression of Indian tribal and social and religious institutions," see "A New Deal for the American Indian," *The Literary Digest* (April 7, 1934), 21 (Accessed online at http://www.unz.org/ on

March 22, 2017).

53. Brian F. Rader, "Oklahoma Indian Welfare Act," *The Encyclopedia of Oklahoma History and Culture*, www.okhistory.org (accessed March 22, 2017).

54. The Oklahoma Indian Welfare Act, June 26, 1936 (Thomas-Rogers Act), Senate Bill 2074, Public Law 816. Oklahoma Indian Welfare Act (1936) 74th Congress, Session II, Chapter 831, p 1976 GSA. Brian F. Rader, "Oklahoma Indian Welfare Act," *Encyclopedia of Oklahoma History and Culture*, www.okhistory.org (accessed March 18, 2016).

55. Constitution of the Miami Tribe of Oklahoma, 1939. In 1996, the Miami Tribe amended its constitution to rename the gender specific council position a more representative and gender-neutral title: Councilperson.

56. Deed of sale United States Government to George E. Nicholson, filed 23 April 1903.

57. In 1976, the Inter-Tribal Council (ITC) of Northeast Oklahoma consisted of eight tribes. In 2000, the ITC was expanded to nine as the Shawnee Tribe was re-recognized separately from the Cherokee Nation.

58. 2014 Annual Report of the Miami Tribe of Oklahoma: Presented to the General Council, June 7, 2014, 19.

Maps

Figure 1: Riverine map of Myaamionki by Brett Governanti and Joshua Sutterfield.

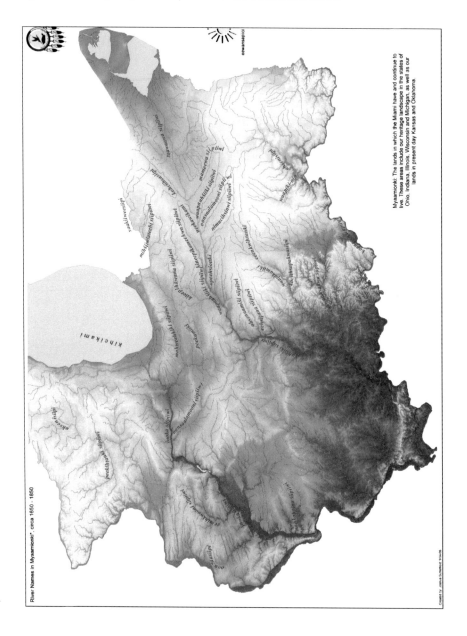

Figure 2: Map depicting the removal route of the Miami Nation in the fall of 1846.

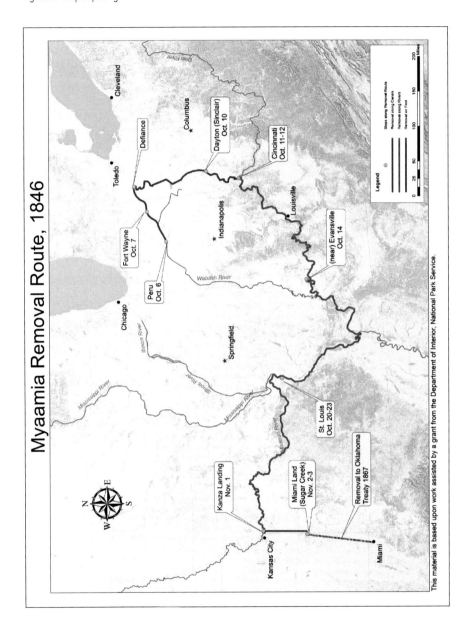

Figure 3: Miami Tribe of Oklahoma allotment map by Brad Kasberg. In this map all sixty-six Miami allotments are depicted and color-coded to show family grouping.

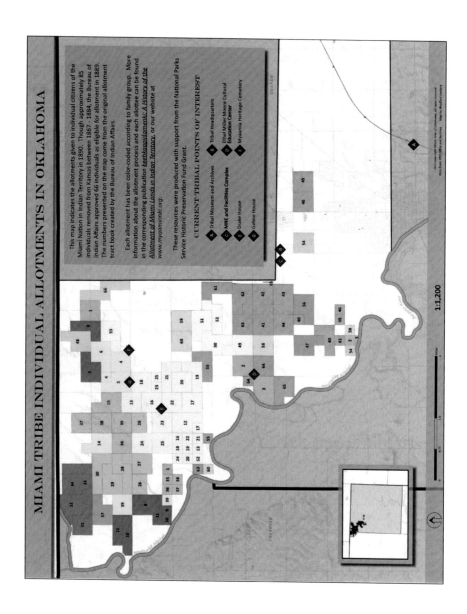

Figure 4: Below is the key to the allotment map. The allottee listing is organized by allotment number, as is the biography section of this publication. The allotments are color coded on the map according to family groups.

ALLOTEE IDENTIFICATION

1	John Miller	34	Columbus Bright
2	Esther Miller Dagenett	35	George W. Leonard
3	Lewis W. Miller	36	Charles W. Leonard
4	David Geboe	37	Helen Leonard Sims
5	Mary Bridget Leonard Geboe	38	Barbara 'Anna' Leonard Murry Schultz
6	Minnie Geboe Trinkle	39	Louisa Geboe Leonard
7	Oscar LaFalier	40	Thomas F. Richardville
8	Henry LaFalier	41	Mary Lindsey Richardville
9	Mary 'Necy' LaFalier Gobin	42	Hannah Richardville McManaman
10	David LaFalier	43	Catherine Richardville Simpson
11	Jessie LaFalier Younglood	44	Charles W. Richardville
12	William 'Wayne' Drake	45	Lizzie Lindsey Palmer
13	Louisa Drake Roseberry	46	Thomas Hartley Palmer
14	Lucy Josephine 'Josie' Geboe Paup Fulkerson	47	Charles S. Welch
15	Mary Louise Roubidoux Leonard	48	Sophia Roubidoux Bluejacket Goodboo LaFalier
16	Jane Pigeon Drake	49	Mary Shapp Wea Buck Daugherty
17	Mary Drake VanDusen	50	Frank Buck, Jr.
18	Josephine 'Josie' Drake Pope	51	Susan Crawfish
19	David H. Drake	52	Luella Isadore Crawfish Beaver Quapaw Wilson
20	Edward Drake	53	Peter Shapp
21	Sarah Drake Horton	54	Lizzie Davis McCoontz
22	Milton D. Drake, Jr.	55	Susan Benjamin Medicine
23	John L. Drake	56	Isadora Labadie Smith
24	Thomas S. Drake	57	Frank D. Aveline
25	Martha 'Marchie' Drake Hale Runkle	58	Rose Ann Bertrand Kishco Keah
26	Mary Adeline Boure Dollar Billington	59	Lizzie Mahiner Gokey
27	Theodore W. Dollar	60	Joseph Kishco
28	Silver 'Luddie' Dollar Lucas	61	Mary Louise Richardville Pooler
29	Adeline G. Billington Leonard	62	Francis C. 'Frank' Pooler
30	Milton Howard Billington	63	Louis David Pooler
31	Margaret 'Peggy' Davis Bright	64	Rose Ann Richardville Demo
32	John L. Bright	65	Charles M. Demo
33	Florence 'Flora' Bright	66	Edward G. Harris

FAMILY GROUP

Aveline

Benjamin

Billington-Dollar

Bright

Davis

Drake

Geboe

Labadie

LaFalier

Leonard

Mahiner-Kishco

Miller

Richardville

Roubidoux

Shapp

Welch

Part II - Allottee Biographies

Part II - Allottee Biographies

It is undeniable that a nation is strengthened by its citizens working together to maintain their government, culture, and heritage. This is evident at many points in the history of the Miami Nation. The citizens of 1889 are no more or less important than those of 1795 or 1830 or 1939, but we are taking note of them here on an individual basis as a way to provide a snapshot into the circumstances of allotment.

These are people who were greatly impacted by removal, whether they were participants or children of participants or community members who followed thereafter. They are our ancestors and kin, and they kept the Miami Nation fiercely paddling together in our shared mihsooli (canoe) when so many forces were trying to tear us apart. For many Myaamiaki, these individuals serve as the bridge between "history" and "my story." They were not all good, nor were they all bad; they were just people trying to raise families and earn incomes during a difficult time. Some held tightly to their Myaamia identity and passed that pride on to the future generations. Others, for a variety of reasons, did not, but their stories are still important.

The following sixty-six biographies are organized by the original allotment number assigned by the Office of Indian Affairs in 1890. This number corresponds with the allotment map located on pages 46-47. The information contained here presents what we know at the time of publication, and as we continue to study and learn, that information may change. Biographies will also be published online, and additional information such as documents, photos, and corrected information may be found at (www.myaamionki.org).

waahkamiikatwa
John Miller
Born: about 1865 ❖ Died: 27 October 1889

John Miller was the second son of Akima Mihtohseenia (Chief Thomas Miller) and a Myaamia woman named Waapikihkihkwa (also known as Nancy Miller). Unfortunately, John passed away very shortly after the list was taken for allotments, even before he received the patent for his land. He was about 25 years old. It is unlikely John had a wife or children before he died.

aahsansamohkwa
Esther Miller Dagenett
Born: 18 December 1869 ❖ Died: 24 November 1936

Esther Miller was the youngest child born to Akima Mihtohseenia (Chief Thomas Miller) and Waapikihkihkwa. Her mother died when she was about nine years old, after which her father married Almina White, of the Peoria Tribe. Esther was very intelligent, and was a member of the first graduating class at Carlisle Indian School in 1889. Furthering her education, she also graduated from Gem City Business College in 1891. She married Charles E. Dagenett in 1892. Esther was a teacher and matron in the service of the Department of Indian Affairs education system for thirty years, working in such places as Chilocco, Muskogee, Kiowa, and Seneca Indian Schools. Charles was a well-respected agent for the Department, and he

Esther Miller
1889 Graduate of
Carlisle Indian
Industrial School

Photo courtesy Dickinson College Special Collections

and Esther both worked for many years in western states, including Arizona, New Mexico, and Colorado. She and Charles had one daughter, who died at birth. Eventually, they divorced and Esther moved back home to Miami to be with her family.

Esther's allotment land was inherited by her niece and nephews, and passed through the family to Lewis Moore, who donated an acre of it to the Miami Tribe in 1975. In 1977-1978, the tribe used an Indian Action Team Grant through the Bureau of Indian Affairs to build the first tribally-owned building on this land, then called the Miami Tribal Longhouse. This building was not only a tool to train tribal members in construction, but also served as a place for Myaamia people to gather for social and governmental activities. In 2008, the building was renamed the Ethel Miller Moore Cultural Education Center in honor of Chief Lewis Moore's mother, and on September 16, 2014, it was added to the Miami Nation Tribal Historic Properties Register.

Lewis Miller, with his wife,
Mary Emma Dagenett

waakapisia
Lewis William Miller

Born: 1861 ❖ Died: 30 December 1896

Lewis was the eldest child of Akima Mihtohseenia (Chief Thomas Miller) and Waapikihkihkwa. He was born in Kansas, and married three times. He first married Rachel Manley, but had no children. His second wife was Ella McLane, and this union brought forth a son, Albert. Both Ella and Albert were allotted under the Peoria Tribe. Lewis' third wife, Mary Emma Dagenett, was also a member of the Peoria Tribe. She was of Wea descent, the daughter of Edwin Dagenett and granddaughter of Christmas Dagenett. They had three children: Ethel, Clarence, and Lewis Edwin. After Lewis passed away at the age of 35 in 1896, Mary Emma married John King.

Photo courtesy National Anthropological Archives

kitahsaakana
David Geboe

Born: 5 October 1830 ❖ Died: 20 January 1899

One of the eldest members to receive an allotment, David Geboe was born in Kiihkayonki (Fort Wayne, Indiana). He participated in the removal from Myaamionki as a young adult. It is not clear whether his parents Peter and Mary Ann were also removed, but it is likely David traveled with some of his siblings and possibly his mother's siblings. While in Kansas, he first married Mary Abner. They had three sons: Joseph, Simeon, and Ora. Joseph and Ora likely died as children, and Simeon died at 29 years old in Indian Territory. After a divorce from Mary Abner, he married Mary Bridget Leonard and had a daughter, Minnie Mae Geboe.

David Geboe was an integral leader of the Myaamia in a time of uncertainty and upheaval. Along with several other leaders, he traveled to Washington, D.C., to negotiate with the federal government during the treaty period. He grew into a leadership role and was elected chief in 1884, after the Myaamia moved from Kansas to Indian Territory. After his tenure as head chief, he continued to serve as second chief until his death in 1899.

Photo courtesy Twila Trinkle Coger

Mary Bridget Leonard Geboe

Born: 1 October 1853 ❖ Died: 2 February 1935

Mary B. Leonard was born to Moses and Mary (Roubidoux) Leonard in Adrian, Michigan. Her family appears to have settled in Michigan for a period of time before the removal of the Myaamia from Indiana, but then moved southwest to join their relatives in Kansas in the 1860s. Mary was married to David Geboe by Thomas Richardville on October 3, 1869. According to family legend, upon their arrival in Indian Territory, they camped along the Spring River on the Quapaw land before building a permanent home on their allotment. One story is told that while they were there, some Indians from a tribe unfamiliar to them came along. Not being able to communicate with them well, Mary became afraid they would steal her baby, but it soon became apparent that they were only looking for food.

After settling on their allotted land, David Geboe became known as a successful farmer, and "Grandma" Geboe was an enterprising business woman. She took in laundry to earn money, and at one time created a cattle dip and charged ranchers by the head to run their cattle through. Their allotment land and farmhouse passed through five generations of the Geboe family before the Miami Nation purchased it, restored the original portion of the house, and included it on the Tribal Historic Properties Register in 2014.

Minne Mae Geboe Trinkle, pictured
with husband Joseph Lee Trinkle.

Minnie Mae Geboe Trinkle

Born: 6 February 1872 ❖ Died: 30 November 1910

Minnie was born in Kansas but was just an infant when the Myaamia
relocated to Indian Territory. Just as her parents' marriage did a generation
before, Minnie Geboe's marriage to Joseph Lee Trinkle brought two Myaamia
families together. Joseph's parents were Henry Trinkle and Mary Josephine
Bundy. Though Joseph technically agreed to become a United States citizen
(thereby giving up his tribal citizenship) and stay in Kansas, Minnie did not,
so she received an allotment in Indian Territory and the entire family relocated
there. Minnie and Joseph were married in 1888, and they had three children
before his death in 1894. They were Mary "Pearl" (Trinkle) Alsbaugh, Mabel
(Trinkle) Olds, and Ernest Trinkle. Minnie was only 38 years old when she
passed away in 1910. Though the two girls were married by then, Ernest was
fifteen and remained in the care of his grandmother Mary Geboe.

Photo courtesy Gary Parsons, MHMA Collection

Oscar LaFalier

Born: 14 February 1867 ❖ Died: 22 July 1953

Oscar LaFalier was the son of Peter and Mary (Beck) LaFalier. Peter was one of the few who made the removal voyage with the Myaamia from Indiana and again moved from Kansas to Indian Territory. However, he died in 1884, before the individual allotments were made. Peter had nine children, with five receiving Miami allotments. Oscar was the eldest of these five siblings. He was born in Miami County, Kansas, and came with his family to Indian Territory as a young boy. He married Nellie Alexander in 1892 and had two children, Mary Irene and Forrest Lee. The LaFalier's lived in Chetopa, Kansas, for a short time before moving to Miami, Oklahoma. Oscar was a barber by trade and had a shop in the basement of the First National Bank. He officially retired from his barber shop in 1934, after thirty years of business. As a widower, Oscar kept himself busy by selling magazines and publications in the lobby of the Hotel Main and traveling often to visit his son in Amarillo. Oscar also remained active as a leader in the Tribe, serving as secretary for several years. After a flood devastated Miami in 1951, Oscar moved west to Colorado and then on to California to be near his daughter Mary. For a short time, he was a barber at the Beverly Hills Hotel.

Photo courtesy Judy Davis

Chief Judy (Lester) Davis held by her
great-grandfather, Henry LaFalier,
and flanked by her grandfathers
(from left to right) Oscar Stone, Jim
Lester, and Ernest LaFalier, November 1947.

Henry LaFalier

Born: 30 March 1869 ❖ Died: 14 May 1954

Henry was the second son of Peter and Mary LaFalier to be allotted.
After coming to Indian Territory when he was just a small boy, Henry LaFalier
stayed near the family allotment lands the rest of his life. He married Ellie
Webb in 1898, and they had two children, Ernest and Beulah. He and Ellie
divorced in 1910, and Ernest and Beulah remained living with Henry. Both
Ernest and Beulah remained near the original allotment area their entire lives,
and continued the family tradition of farming.

Henry's grandson Frank was killed in a flash flood after a spring tornado in 1954, and Henry was heartbroken. He passed away in his sleep just a
week after Frank's funeral.

Photo courtesy Virginia Hylton Stokes, MHMA Collection

Mary 'Necy' LaFalier Gobin

Born: 28 June 1872 ❖ Died: 21 October 1949

This LaFalier sibling was always known by her nickname "Necy." The daughter of Peter and Mary (Beck) LaFalier, Necy married Harold Gobin in 1893, and had three children: Musa, Raymond, and Marion. Marion was born in 1897 and lived just five days. Harold died six years after they were married, in 1899. Necy never remarried. Between 1910 and 1915, Necy and her daughter Musa moved to Starr Valley, Nevada. Musa met and married Robert Hylton, and the couple soon moved to Eureka, California. It was at this point where mother and daughter separated, Musa to the west and Necy went east. Necy found work in Nebraska as a housekeeper for a short time before returning to Miami. Like her mother, Musa was also widowed at a relatively young age, in the late 1940s. After Robert's death, Musa returned to Ottawa County and lived with Necy until Necy's death in 1949.

Photo courtesy Virginia Hylton Stokes, MHMA Collection

David LaFalier

Born: about 1882 ❖ Died: about 1919

Not much information is known about David LaFalier. David and his sister Jessie were half-siblings to Oscar, Henry, and Necy, having the same father in Peter LaFalier but different mothers. David married a woman named Grace Newlon in 1902, but they appear to have had no children together. David likely passed away shortly after a record in 1918 reports him as a patient at Eastern State Hospital in Vinita, Oklahoma.

Photo courtesy Virginia Hylton Stokes, HMA Collection

Jessie M. LaFalier Youngblood

Born: March 1885 ❖ Died: 1910

The youngest LaFalier sibling, Jessie, was born in Indian Territory in 1885. Her father, Peter, passed away before she was born and very little is known of her mother. She married a man named John S. Youngblood on October 11, 1900. They had a son, Sidney, and a daughter, Rose Ione. Jessie died at just 25 years old, in 1910. Sidney and Rose lived with their father, who moved to Kaw, Oklahoma, and his family remained within that region in Ponca City and Pawhuska, Oklahoma, as well as over the Kansas border in Arkansas City.

Photo courtesy MHMA Collection

soowilencihsia
William Wayne Drake

Born: 16 December 1868 ❖ Died: 28 January 1936

The eldest son of Milton Drake and Siipiihkwa was born just a few years prior to the relocation to Indian Territory. Always known by his middle name, Wayne married Aletha "Birdie" Brandon in 1895. They had four children: Arizona ("Zona"), Moreland, Clarence, and Fred. A farmer by trade, Wayne and his family moved quite a bit, spending several years in Edna, Kansas, but also Parkman, Wyoming, and ended up in Santa Monica, California just a few years before Wayne's death.

Allotment #13

Photo courtesy Gary Parsons, MHMA Collection

pankihšinohkwa
Louisa Drake Roseberry

Born: 17 May 1866 ❖ Died: 12 September 1955

The eldest of the children of Milton and Jane Drake, Louisa married Joseph Edward "Ed" Roseberry and had two children: Thomas and Jane. Ed was a cattleman, and the family moved between 1910 and 1915 to Kansas City, where he worked for the Stockyards. During the Depression, they went to Holly, Colorado, again to find work in the cattle industry. Louisa remained in Colorado until her death in 1955.

Lucy Josephine 'Josie' Geboe Paup Fulkerson
Born: 23 August 1862 ❖ Died: 1939

Josie Geboe was the daughter of Elias Geboe and Mary Ann Hoggatt, but both her parents died when she was a young girl. Josie had a short-lived marriage in 1879 to a man named S. Paup. In 1884, she married Fent Fulkerson. They moved to Beowawe, Nevada, shortly thereafter, where Fent was a ranch superintendent. They never had any children and lived out the rest of their lives in Nevada. She sold most of her allotted land in 1902.

Allotment #15

Mary Louisa Roubidoux Leonard

Born: 4 September 1830 ❖ Died: 28 February 1894

Mary Louisa Roubidoux was born on the reserve of her grandmother Josette Beaubien, near Fort Wayne, Indiana. She was the sister of Eecipoonkwia (John Baptiste Roubidoux), who would become chief of the Miami Nation in Kansas. It appears that her family moved north and settled in Michigan for a period of time prior to the removal of the Myaamia from Indiana. This move was possibly caused by the death of her father Joseph Roubidoux in 1842. While there, in 1851, she married Moses Leonard. In the 1860s, Mary and Moses rejoined their relatives in Kansas, where she and her children were allotted land. Their daughter Mary Bridget Leonard married David Geboe and received her own allotment. One of the eldest allottees, Mary Louisa died just a few years after the allotment process was completed.

siipiihkwa
Jane Pigeon Drake

Born: between 1845-1850 ❖ Died: 29 July 1918

Photo courtesy Gary Parsons, MHMA Collection

It is unclear where Jane was born, and her exact familial relationships to other Myaamia are not certain. It is possible her family was part of the band of Myaamia who fled to Michigan in order to evade the forced removal from Indiana. It is also uncertain how or when she came to Kansas. What is known is that she received an allotment in Kansas, and married Milton K. Drake on that land in 1866. Milton and Jane had twelve children, eleven of whom received allotments in Indian Territory. The youngest son of Milton and Jane, and the only child not to receive an allotment, Patrick, was only twelve years old when he died from typhoid fever in 1909.

The Drakes built what is now known simply as "The Drake House" on Jane's parcel around 1895 and the family continued to farm the land until about 1920. Milton died in a buggy accident in 1905, and Jane fought to keep the farm successful until her death in 1918, but it was not easy. Eventually the farm had to be sold, but the house remained standing and was bought and restored by the Miami Nation in 2005. As one of the few remaining houses from the allotment period, it was placed on the Miami Nation Register of Historic Places in 2006.

Photo courtesy Gary Parsons, MHMA Collection

kihcikamiihkwa
Mary Drake VanDusen

Born: about 1871 ❖ Died: 28 October 1903

The first of the children of Milton and Jane Drake to be born after the Myaamia relocation to Indian Territory, Mary married George VanDusen, a cabinet-maker who had emigrated from Canada, on December 28, 1898. She and George had three daughters: Mabel, Ida, and Marchie. Mary died when Marchie was an infant, at just 32 years old. In 1909, George married a woman named Jennie Clark who helped raise the girls in Baxter Springs, Kansas.

Photo courtesy MHMA Collection

oonseentiihkwa
Josephine 'Josie' Drake Pope

Born: 28 February 1872 ❖ Died: 19 July 1958

Though the Drake family is well known for their homeplace on Jane Drake's allotment, Josie's recorded birthplace was Chetopa, Kansas, just across the state border to the north. It is quite possible they retained a residence there until the farmhouse construction was complete. Josie Drake married John Adams Pope in Miami on September 3, 1895. They had three sons, Milton Bismark, John A., Jr., and Douglas. The Pope family moved to Texas around 1900. John Pope was a lawyer and his sons followed in his footsteps of practicing law. All three sons served in the military during World War I. Douglas tragically died in an accidental drowning when he was 26, but the descendants of John and Milton Bismark Pope still live in Texas.

mihšahkatwa
David H. Drake
Born: 25 December 1874 ❖ Died: unknown

A lifelong bachelor, David Drake worked as a ranch hand and cowboy in several different locations across Indian Territory. Family stories suggest he may have even jumped rail cars for a period of time. The last known official record of David's life is found on the 1937 tribal roll, where he was recorded as 62 years old and living in Fairfax, Osage County, Oklahoma.

Photo courtesy MHMA Collection

mihtekia
Edward Drake

Born: 14 November 1875 ❖ Died: 21 July 1944

Like his brother-in-law, Ed Roseberry, Edward Drake was drawn to the cattle industry. By 1910, he had sold most of his allotment and moved his family from Oklahoma to El Paso, Texas, and then on to Pinal County, Arizona, where they lived for over 25 years. Edward was married to Susie Mitchell and had two children: Thomazine Dorma and Theos Pope. Another son, Alwyn Wayne, died as an infant while still in Oklahoma.

Photo courtesy MHMA Collection

kocenohkwa
Sarah Drake Horton

Born: 15 April 1878 ❖ Died: 15 July 1966

Eager to leave the Drake Farm where she was raised, Sarah married Charles E. Horton in 1902. They had just one child, Kenneth. Though she didn't travel as far as some of her siblings, Sarah and her family moved between 1905 and 1910 to McPherson, Stephens County, Oklahoma, then to Hugo, Oklahoma. Sarah was living in Oklahoma City in 1966 when she died.

Photo courtesy MHMA Collection

Milton Dyer Drake, Jr.

Born: 21 August 1883 ❖ Died: unknown

Milton Drake, Jr., married Carrie Rolater in 1907, and had a son, Milton "Johnnie" Drake born in 1909. Unfortunately, his young namesake passed away in 1911. For a short time around 1918, he worked at the stockyards in Chicago; but returned home in due time. Milton divorced Carrie around 1919 and married Cynthia Jane Dobson. They had five children: James, Jessee, Estalee, Milton, and Hazel. By 1930, he was living in Chickasha, Oklahoma, while working on a farm. He is found in the historical record again, for the last time, on the 1940 federal census, living in Weatherford, Oklahoma, at the age of fifty-seven.

Photo courtesy Gary Parsons, MHMA Collection

John Drake (right) pictured with his son, Teddy, and niece, Ida VanDusen.

John Logan Drake

Born: 27 April 1884 ❖ Died: 22 April 1967

John Logan Drake married Della Leonard, another Miami allottee, on May 17, 1909, in Commerce. They had four children: John, Paul (known by his nickname "Teddy"), Wayne Logan, and Geraldine. John, Jr., died as a young boy, and Wayne died in the service of this country during World War II. John farmed in Ottawa County until the late 1920s, when he moved to Kansas City and worked in the Stockyards.

Teddy Drake remembered the Drake Farm fondly, and painted a scene as he remembered it from his boyhood, which is now at the Myaamia Heritage Museum and Archive.

Photo courtesy June Drake Hanna

Thomas Sumner Drake

Born: 18 April 1887 ❖ Died: March 1961

Like several others in the family, Thomas Drake farmed in Ottawa County until the late 1920s, and then moved to Kansas City to work in the Stockyards. He married Beatrice June Leach and together they had nine children: Vernon, Jane, Nadene, Bonnie, Maurice, Jean, Betty, Thomas, and Iona. Coincidentally, Beatrice was Angie Leach Billington's sister, so Howard Billington's daughters and Tom Drake's children are first cousins. Many of his descendants still live in the Kansas City area. His daughter Iona Learned is now 83 years old and living in Manhattan, Kansas.

Photo courtesy Brooke Evans Eastburn

Martha 'Marchie' Drake Hale Runkle

Born: 13 January 1888 ❖ Died: 16 December 1984

The youngest Drake girl was always known by her nickname "Marchie." She married John S. Hale, a lawyer, in 1907. After the birth of their daughter Jewell in 1908, the family seemed to be on the rise in Miami, when John ran into trouble later that year. According to a short notice in the *Miami News-Herald*, he was arrested for impersonating a federal officer and was held at the Muskogee, Oklahoma, jail. After he was found guilty, the family moved away from Miami for a fresh start. John Hale returned to law after a short time, practicing in Muskogee by 1912. John was 23 years older than Marchie, and it is unclear what happened to him thereafter, but by 1920, Marchie was married to W. W. Runkle and living in Hugo, Oklahoma. She was living in Oklahoma City when she passed away in 1984.

Mary Adeline is seated in the
rocking chair.

maankoonsihkwa
Mary Adeline Boure Dollar Billington

Born: September 1853 ❖ Died: 18 December 1933

Mary Adeline was the daughter of John Baptiste Boure, Jr., and Roseann Geboe, the sister of Chief David Geboe. Family stories say that John Boure, Jr., left for better opportunities on the western frontier in the late 1850s and was never heard from again. Mary Adeline's mother, Roseann, later married John Sharkey and had one other son. Mary Adeline married Winchell Theodore Dollar, a Dutch immigrant, in about 1868 while still in Kansas. They had several children, but only two, Theodore and Silver, lived out of childhood. Mary Adeline divorced Mr. Dollar and married Asariah Billington in about 1883. They had four more children: Addie, Milton Howard, Rose Ann, and Frank. All told, by 1900, Mary Adeline had given birth to 13 children, but only 6 were then living. After a life of such hardship and loss, it is easy to believe the family stories that portray Mary Adeline as a "feisty" woman, handy with a pipe and shotgun.

Allotment #27

Theodore W. Dollar

Born: 4 January 1875 ❖ Died: 1958

The fourth child born to W. T. and Mary Adeline Dollar, Theodore was born at the beginning of 1875. A sister, Elie, had died five months earlier, and by the end of the year, Theodore would be the only child living. Theodore's family allotments were in the northwestern part of the Miami lands, but they resided north of the Kansas border near Chetopa. Around the turn of the century, Theodore married Avis Byers. Together, they had four children: Mary Elizabeth, Francis T., Thomas Woodrow, and Bert Glen Dollar. The family moved to Enid, Oklahoma, and later Tulsa, and lived in California for many years but Theodore moved back home after separating from his wife. Upon his return, he served as a Tribal Councilperson in 1938, while the Tribe was in the process of creating and approving the first Tribal Constitution. Many of Theodore's descendants still live in California and other parts of the West Coast.

Photo courtesy MHMA Collection

Silver 'Luddie' Dollar Lucas
Born 16 February 1877 ❖ Died: 22 October 1951

It is said that Silver Dollar received her name because she was born on "annuity day." When the agent asked what name he should write down on the payroll, her father said "Silver." Her mother owned a hotel in Miami, and that is where Silver met her husband, Otho 'Doc' Lucas. They were married in 1900 and moved to her mother's allotted land, but Doc wasn't much of a farmer so they soon moved to Chetopa, Kansas. They welcomed their first child, Amber, in 1901, followed in quick order by Marie, Edward, Katherine, Ada Lucille, Mary, and Edna. Edward, their only son, died at just four months old, in 1905. They also lost their daughter Amber, son-in-law Adren Evans, and their granddaughter Norma Jean Evans to a car accident in 1948. Silver Dollar was known for her good disposition and great laugh. She is remembered for her strong Christian faith, the generosity she showed to all, and for the long hair she always kept in a braid, but most of all for the love she had for her large family. She and Doc left a great legacy for the five children and twenty-one grandchildren that came after them.

Adeline, right, pictured with her
sister Rosa Billington Beck.

Adeline G. Billington Leonard

Born: 14 March 1884 ❖ Died: 11 April 1971

Adeline "Addie" Billington was the first child of Asariah Billington and Mary Adeline (Boure) Dollar. She attended school at the Quapaw Boarding School, Chetopa Public School, and Chilocco Indian School before returning home and marrying Charles W. Leonard, another Miami allottee. Addie and Charles had nine children, and twenty-one grandchildren. Addie proudly raised her children (Irene, Elmer, Carl, Busey, Cora, LeRoy, Anna, Everett Eugene, and Verdenia Pauline), but she was also very proud of her grandchildren. After Charles' death in 1940, Addie spent a great deal of her time with the grandchildren, and taught them their Myaamia heritage. The Quapaw Indian Competency Commission interviewed both her and Charles in 1910, as part of the process of removing restrictions on selling allotted land. The commissioner's record gives an impression of a family living with humble means, struggling to support their family in hard economic times. But it also says they were educated, robust, and industrious. They knew the meaning of hard work, and passed that on to their family.

Milton Howard Billington

Born: 20 May 1886 ❖ Died: 5 June 1912

Howard married Angie (Moore) Leach on April 18, 1908, in Miami. They had two daughters, Wilmah 'Juanita' and Hilda Faye. Unfortunately, Howard died at the young age of 26. His daughters were only two years and seven months old at the time, respectively. However, many of his descendants have carried on his Myaamia legacy and have stayed involved with the tribe.

seekaahkohkwa
Margaret 'Peggy' Davis Bright
Born: between 1846-1853 ❖ Died: after 1920

Peggy Bright is most likely the daughter of a man known as John We-oxie, who may have been Potawatomi, and a Myaamia woman named Mihšah-katohkwa, born very soon after the removal from Indiana, perhaps as early as 1846 but more likely closer to 1850. Her mother later married Jim Davis (e-to-wah-ke-sic). The records are inconsistent regarding her family, but it is likely she was considered a ward in need of guardianship while still a minor. She married James Wesley Bright while the Miami Nation still resided in Kansas, and their children were John, Flora, Columbus, Josie, Frankie, and Fredonia. Frankie and Josie passed away before allotments were made, leaving John, Flora, and Columbus to receive allotments.

John L. Bright

Born: about 1870 ❖ Died: unknown

It seems that bad fortune followed John most his life. He married Dolly McFarlin, and they had a daughter, Velma Francis Bright, born in 1892. The little one died at just two years old, followed by her young mother in 1900. By 1910, John had been married and divorced again, to Nettie Rollen. He is last found in the records at age 40, as an inmate at the McAlester (Oklahoma) Penitentiary, charged with assault with intent to kill, after threatening to shoot his father. No living descendants of John Bright are known.

mihšahkatohkwa
Florence 'Flora' Bright

Born: 28 September 1875 ❖ Died: 10 February 1907

Flora Bright lived in her parents' household her whole life. She was given her grandmother's Myaamia name, though many Myaamia born at this time had only English names. She was never married and died at the age of 32.

awansaapia
Columbus Bright

Born: 2 May 1888 ❖ Died: 5 March 1960

One of the youngest allottees, Columbus married Bessie Charley (Peoria) on Christmas Day, 1908. They had four children: Violet, William, Margaret, and Columbus. After his divorce in 1917, Columbus had one more son, Paul Eugene, born in 1922. Columbus was an Army Veteran, serving at Camp Pike, Arkansas during World War I. He moved around quite a bit after his military service, spending time in Pawhuska, Oklahoma and Kansas City, Missouri. He was living in Norman, Oklahoma when he died in 1960.

Allotment #35

George Washington Leonard
Born: 22 February 1857 ❖ Died: 28 October 1919

George Washington Leonard was the son of Moses and Mary Louisa (Roubidoux) Leonard, and the sister to Mary Bridget (Leonard) Geboe. George was born in Adrian, Michigan but received a land allotment in Kansas and moved there with his family while he was still a young boy. In 1877, he married Cynthia Sigman and had a son, Charles, in 1879. He and Cynthia had another son, named Clarence, who was born in 1880, and a third boy who died as an infant in 1882. Cynthia passed away early in 1883, and Clarence died the following spring, at only three years old.

George Leonard,
with his wife,
Cynthia Sigman Leonard.

George married Minniehaha Wade in 1884. Minnie's father Andrew J. Wade was a doctor who worked closely with the Indians residing around Paola, Kansas, and her mother's ancestry reached back to President John Adams. George and Minnie had eight children together; six girls and two boys. The eldest was Helen, born in 1885, and the youngest, Hazel, came in 1900. Helen's younger sister Barbara Anna received an allotment, but the next girl in line, Della, was born just a few months after the cut-off date. Their brothers were Harry and Earl, both of whom died at young ages. Carrie was born next, followed by Nellie. Nellie also died at just over a year old. Minnie (Wade) Leonard died at age 43, in 1904. Following her death, George had two other short-lived marriages.

For a short period of time, George was employed as a police officer for the Indian Agency, but primarily lived as a farmer, particularly after allotments were made. The Leonard allotment tracts were north and just slightly west of where the Drake House now stands.

Photo courtesy Clarence Hayward

Charles W. Leonard

Born: 24 February 1879 ❖ Died: 20 June 1940

Bringing two Miami families together, Addie Billington and Charles Leonard were married February 26, 1900. Charles was the son of George W. Leonard and Cynthia Sigman and the grandson of Moses Leonard and Marie Louisa Roubidoux. Before marrying, Charles had attended Haskell Indian School in Kansas, and Addie had graduated from Chilocco Indian School. It was not long after their respective educations that they married. Charles and Addie's marriage brought forth five sons and four daughters: Irene, Elmer Charles, Carl Edgar, Busey, Cora, LeRoy, Anna Rose, Everett Eugene, and Verdenia Pauline. The Leonard family operated a farm near Chetopa, Kansas just north of their allotted land.

Allotment #37

Photo courtesy James Sims Collection, MS9, MHMA

Helen Mae Leonard Sims

Born: 12 January 1885 ❖ Died: 24 April 1958

Helen grew up in Ottawa County as the oldest child of George and Minnie Leonard. She married Frank Sims in 1904 and surely loved being a caretaker. They had a large family of eleven children: Ray, Roy, Pearl Minnie, Oscar, Esther, Anna, Ruth, James, Hazel, Buford, and Ramona.

Helen's husband Frank was a farm worker for several years but later the family moved into Miami, where he found jobs as a laborer. A report in the *Miami News-Record* in August of 1928 tells of the tragic death of Frank and Helen's son Oscar, who died from injuries after he was gored by a bull in Arthur, Nebraska. He was only nineteen years old. Helen passed away in 1958 and was buried just north of her family's allotments, in Melrose, Kansas. Her youngest daughter Ramona (Sims) Brubaker passed away in 2013. Before his death in 2011, Helen's son James gave the tribal archives some photos of his family, including a photo of Helen. Also included in the tribal archive collections are some photos from her daughter Hazel, who served for several years in the Women's Army Corps.

Photo courtesy Deborah Langford Collection, MS 6, MHMA

Barbara 'Anna' Leonard Murray Schultz

Born: 20 January 1887 ❖ Died: 20 January 1963

Not much is known about Anna's life. She was married and divorced and lived in Kansas City, Missouri for most of her adult life. The 1940 Census notes that she worked as a seamstress in a garment factory and lived with her sister Della's family.

Samuel and Louisa Geboe Leonard.

Photo courtesy Sammye Leonard Darling, MC 3, MHMA Collection

Louisa Geboe Leonard

Born: 1872 ❖ Died: 1918

Louisa was the daughter of Michael M. Geboe, a Civil War veteran, and Nancy Childres. Her father never fully recovered from the war and claimed disability after returning to Kansas. He passed away August 19, 1877, leaving Louisa an orphan at only five years old. She was raised in the household of her relative Akima Kitahsaakana (Chief David Geboe). She married Samuel Alfred Leonard in Columbus, Kansas on August 1, 1891. Their first son James Wilbur ("Leggy") was born in 1892, followed by Gabriel ("Gib"), Joseph ("Hike"), Ruby, Martha Pearl, David ("Bus"), Grace, Mabel, Samuel, Hansel, Donald, Minnie ("Beezy"), and Henry. Louisa died at the young age of 46. Just about all the Leonard boys worked in the lead and zinc mines of Picher, and some descendants later moved to Washington, Idaho, and Ohio.

waapimaankwa
Thomas Francis Richardville

Born: 23 April 1830 ❖ Died: 16 January 1911

Waapimaankwa was the great-grandson of Akima Pinšiwa (Chief J. B. Richardville), the son of a man known as Pimicinwa or Crescent Richardville. Thomas was orphaned at a young age and grew up in Indiana. Though he was exempted from removal and did not make the trip to Kansas Territory in 1846, he rejoined his Myaamia community in the Spring of 1860. Chief Richardville had eight children by three wives. His oldest children were Francis, Rose Ann, Mary Louisa and Mary Jane, all of whom came from his first marriage to Angeline Good-boo. In 1866, he married Ruth Ozandiah and had a son Henry Moses. He later married Martonah (Mary Lindsey) and had three children: Catherine, Charles, and Hannah. Educated as a lawyer at Notre Dame, he became a valuable intermediary between the Miami Nation and the United States government. Though he was influential in leadership for many years prior, he first became Chief in 1888, after the relocation to Indian Territory. Chief Richardville's leadership was integral to the decision to remain a separate entity upon relocation, rather than consolidating membership with the Peoria Tribe as allowed under the 1867 Treaty.

Photo courtesy National Anthropological Archives

martonah
Mary Lindsey Richardville

Born: April 1839 ❖ Died: 25 January 1908

Born before the removal from Indiana, Martonah's exact ancestry is un-confirmed, though it appears she was a relative of Charles Welch and that her family came from the Eel River village in Indiana. She received an allotment in Kansas when she was married to Marcus Lindsey. After Mr. Lindsey's death in 1867, Martonah married Thomas Richardville in Paola, Kansas. Together, they had three children: Hannah, Catherine, and Charles. About ten years her elder, Thomas outlived Mary by just three years; she was sixty-nine years old when she passed.

kiišikohkwa
Hannah Richardville McManaman

Born: 24 March 1872 ❖ Died: 14 August 1902

    The eldest daughter of Thomas and Mary Richardville, Hannah was well educated and served as secretary for the Tribe under her father's leadership as Chief. She married Levi McManaman, a teacher, in 1892 and died just ten years later. She did not have any children.

šinkohkwa
Catherine Richardville Simpson
Born: 29 March 1875 ❖ Died: about 1914

Catherine "Katie" Richardville, along with her brother Charles, attended school at Bacone Indian University in Muskogee, Oklahoma. She married John B. Simpson in 1904. Her husband worked as a farmer, likely on or near the Richardville allotment land. Mrs. Simpson was noted in records as being "intelligent, industrious, and capable." She did not have any children and, like her sister Hannah, died at a relatively young age.

Photo courtesy Jim & Jean Richardville

eeloonoonta
Charles Woodson Richardville

Born: 31 March 1877 ❖ Died: 16 February 1932

Charles, the youngest child of Thomas and Mary Richardville, grew up in Indian Territory and spent most of his life as a mortician and undertaker. For several years, he worked in Webb City and Joplin, Missouri and later in life, in Colorado Springs. He returned to Joplin just two months before his death in 1932. He and his wife, Marie Martin, had one son, Thomas, born in 1903.

waapimaankohkwa
Elizabeth 'Lizzie' Lindsey Palmer

Born: 5 May 1860 ❖ Died: unknown

Lizzie Lindsey was the daughter of Martonah (Mary) and Marcus Lindsey. Martonah was a Myaamia woman and Marcus Lindsey was of Peoria descent. After Marcus died in 1867, Martonah married Thomas F. Richardville. Lizzie Lindsey married James Palmer in 1880. Mr. Palmer was an instrumental figure in establishing the town of Miami and was its first postmaster. In 1881, Lizzie gave birth to their only child, Thomas Harley Palmer. Lizzie and Harley's allotted land was located the farthest east of any Miami allotments, near the current-day G.A.R. Cemetery. When the Quapaw Agency Competency Commissioners interviewed Mrs. Palmer in 1910, they found her and her family to be "in prosperous condition." The family continued to live in Miami until James Palmer's death in 1936. By 1940, Lizzie was living with her grandson Moody Palmer's family in Fort Washakie, Wyoming. Her whereabouts thereafter are unknown.

katakimaankwa
Thomas Harley Palmer

Born: 22 July 1881 ❖ Died: 28 January 1965

Photo courtesy MHMA Collection

Harley Palmer was born in 1881, the son of James L. Palmer and Lizzie Lindsey. He grew up in Indian Territory, near his mother's Richardville family. He married Ada Moore on December 31, 1901. Ada was of Peoria and Wea descent, the daughter of Mary Isabelle (Labadie) Moore. Through this connection, Ada was a first cousin of another Myaamia allottee, Isadore (Labadie) Smith. Harley and Ada had eight children: Moody, Maxine, Woody, Louise, Mary, James, Gloria, and Blossom. Harley succeeded his step-grandfather Thomas F. Richardville as Chief in 1910, at the young age of 27. He went on to serve for fifty-three years, overseeing many major changes in the administration of the Miami Nation. At the beginning of his time as Chief, the nation was still under the jurisdiction of the Quapaw Agency, but that was discontinued in 1921. Many tribal members have recalled Chief Palmer visiting their farms on horseback to talk to them. After the Oklahoma Indian Welfare Act of 1936, Chief Palmer had the foresight to fight for the continued self-determination of the Miami Nation by overseeing the ratification of the first Tribal Constitution in 1939. He also led the Miami Tribe's early efforts before the Indian Claims Commission, which eventually secured individual payments for tribal members. He continued to serve in tribal government until 1963, when Forest Olds was elected as Chief.

pimihsia
Charles S. Welch
Born: 1853 ❖ Died: 30 October 1897

Though he was born after removal, very little is known about Charles Welch's background. Probate records suggest that his mother may have been a Myaamia woman whose name was recorded as "Ne-pe-ah-kah", and he may have been directly related to Martonah (Mary Richardville). A few years after he was born, Ne-pe-ah-kah married a Myaamia man named Kiilhsoonsa (Snap Richardville). Snap was the grandson of Akima Pinšiwa (Chief Jean B. Richardville) and although exempted from removal, it appears that he participated in the removal journey south to the Miami Reservation in 1846.

In 1884, Charles married Sarah Martin, the step-daughter of Peter Lafalier, better known by her other married name, Sarah Wadsworth. They had no known children, and he later married a Peoria woman named Sallie Wasacolly (or Wasacoleah). They had two children, Thomas and Benjamin. Thomas received a Peoria allotment but died when he was just eighteen years old. However, Benjamin remained connected to both the Miami and Peoria Tribes throughout his life.

Charles Welch served as a Councilperson from at least 1879 to 1884 when he was elected as Second Chief of the Nation. Her served as Second Chief until 1887 when he resigned halfway through his second term, nominating Waapimaankwa (Thomas Richardville) to replace him. After stepping down from that position, he served again as a Councilperson until his death in 1897. He is buried in the eastern "historic section" of the current Tribal Cemetery.

Photo courtesy Barbara Mullin

Sophia Viola Roubidoux Bluejacket Goodboo LaFalier

Born: about 1864 ❖ Died: 25 July 1925

Sophia was the youngest daughter of Akima Eecipoonkwia (Chief John Baptiste Roubidoux) and his wife Susan. She was raised in Paola, Kansas, until the Myaamia relocated to Indian Territory. Her first husband was named Moses Bluejacket. They had no children, and around 1888 she married Thomas Goodboo, a Miami and Potawatomi man who was born and raised in Indiana. They had six children, three boys and three girls. Mary was the eldest, followed by Ethel, Frank, Allen, Josephine, and Thomas, Jr. Following Thomas' death in 1899, Sophia married Homer C. LaFalier in 1900. Homer LaFalier was also Miami through his father, Louis LaFalier, but was enrolled in the Cherokee Nation through his matrilineal line (his mother being Sarah Wheeler). Homer and Sophia had four children: John, Louis, Ruby and Homer.

Photo courtesy Quapaw Tribal Library, 1974 Quapaw Pow Wow Program.

pankihšinohkwa or kiilhsoohkwa
Mary Shapp Wea Buck Daugherty
Born: 1858 ❖ Died: 2 December 1942

Mary Shapp was the daughter of John Shapp and Mihšiiminaapowa. She was married first to William Wea and had a son who died as a young toddler in the early 1880s. In the late 1880s, she married Frank Buck, a Quapaw Indian, and had another son, named Frank Buck, Jr. Frank, Sr., passed away in 1899, and in 1903, Mary married Howard Daugherty. After she became a widow once again in 1923, she remained busy in social affairs and often traveled to see family. When she passed away at the Claremore Indian Hospital at the age of 84, she had outlived most of her family, her son having died two years before her.

Photo courtesy Quapaw Tribal Library, 1974 Quapaw Pow Wow Program.

Frank Buck, Jr.

Born: 28 March 1888 ❖ Died: 28 August 1940

Frank maintained his citizenship in the Miami Nation based on his mother's ancestry. He married Josie Decker about 1908 and had a son, Leonard F. Buck, who also died in 1940. As the heir to his father's Quapaw allotment, Frank benefited from mining leases facilitated thereupon. This afforded him many opportunities to travel but also made him a target for lawsuits. A veteran of World War I, he was a leader in the local American Legion, often attending conventions within the state and across the country with his son. He worked for a time as a farmer in Ottawa County but moved to Los Angeles shortly before his death in 1940. He is buried in the G.A.R. Cemetery in Miami.

Allotment #51

Susan 'Susette' Crawfish
Born: about 1863 ❖ Died: 11 September 1928

The daughter of Martin Luther and Mihšiiminaapowa, Susan was the half-sister of Mary Shapp (Pankihšinohkwa) and John Shapp (Awansaapia). She married Thomas Crawfish and had ten children, but only four were living in 1910: Luella Isadore (Mihšiiminaapowa), Mary, Minnie, and Lucy. Isadore was the only child living at the time allotments were made. Thomas Crawfish's family was Quapaw, and today many of his and Susan's descendants are citizens of the Quapaw Tribe of Oklahoma.

Photo courtesy Quapaw Tribal Library,
1966 Quapaw Pow Wow Program.

mihšiiminaapowa
Luella Isadore Crawfish Beaver Quapaw Wilson
Born: 21 March 1882 ❖ Died: 15 October 1970

Luella Isadore Crawfish was born to Thomas and Susan Crawfish in Indian Territory and lived in the Quapaw and Peoria area all her life. She was married three times: to Alexander Lewis Beaver (1900), Solomon Quapaw (about 1909), and Reed Wilson (sometime after 1924). Isadore always maintained her citizenship in the Miami Nation, but her children were all counted as citizens of their fathers' tribe, the Quapaw Tribe of Oklahoma. Her children by Beaver were Amos, Victor, Mary Francis, and Orville. Her children by Quapaw were Luella B., Elmer Thomas, Cecilia, James Henry, Edward L., and Maude E.

Peter Shapp with his wife,
Julia Stafford Shapp (Quapaw).

waakamwa
Peter Shapp

Born: 17 September 1875 ❖ Died: 21 June 1934

By the time the United States began enumerating Native Americans annually through the Indian Census Rolls in 1885, Peter Shapp was listed on the Miami Roll as an orphan. His father, believed to be John Shapp, appears to have died around 1881, and his mother Jane (Gokey) Shapp passed sometime shortly thereafter. It is likely that John Shapp was a son of John Shapp and Mihšiiminaapowa, making Peter a nephew of Susan Crawfish and Mary Buck. Since he is nearly always listed adjacent to Susan or Mary on tribal census rolls, it is likely they cared for him while he was a boy. Though his grave marker notes a birth date of 1875, earlier records imply he was born as early as 1870, and his given birthplace alternates as Kansas and Oklahoma, so he may have been born very near the time of removal of the Myaamia to Indian Territory.

Peter was married to Julia Stafford on March 14, 1894, by Thomas Richardville. Julia was a Quapaw tribal member, and their nine children were also citizens of the Quapaw Tribe. The Shapp family lived on the Quapaw land near Spring River, and many Shapp descendants still live in that area today. Their first son, John, passed away as a toddler. This was followed by the births of Mary, Harry, Thomas, Urban, Francis, Christina, Flossie Merla, and Charles.

Photo courtesy Leroy J. McCoontze

pankihšinohkwa
Lizzie Davis Thompson McCoontz

Born: about 1871 ❖ Died: 2 January 1910

Though Lizzie's allotment card states that her mother was also named Lizzie Davis, she was listed as a ward or orphan from very early on in her life. In 1890, Milton Drake was serving as her guardian, and she was also often associated with the Shapp family. Mary Shapp may have also served as a guardian. Around 1893, she married a man named John Thompson. She had two sons, Joseph Thompson and Willie Buffalo Thompson. However, both died as children. She later married an Ottawa Indian, Peter McCoontz, and had four more sons: John, James, Joseph, and Francis. None of her children were born before allotments were made.

awanohkamihkwa
Susan Benjamin Medicine
Born: between 1847-1850 ❖ Died: 1911

Susan was born in Kansas shortly after the removal from Indiana. Her allotment card states that she was the sister to Thomas Miller's first wife, Waapihkihkihkwa. Though their exact parents are unknown, Susan and Waapihkihkihkwa were the heirs to the Beaver Reserve in Indiana, a contested case that followed them all the way to Indian Territory. Susan was married to John Benjamin (Soowilencihsia), and they had three children who were not allotted; it is likely all three died as young children. John also died before arriving in Indian Territory. She later married a Quapaw man named John Medicine (sometimes recorded as Madison) but had no children with him.

kiilhsoohkwa
Isadora Labadie Smith

Born: 8 July 1870 ❖ Died: 1948

In an interview in 1937, Isadora Smith states that her mother's name was Susan Bigleg, but that she knew "nothing of her life, as she died as I was born and I was taken and reared by my grandparents." Isadora's father was Charles Labadie, and her paternal grandparents were Peter and Umilla Labadie. She

Isadora Labadie Smith, with her husband, Thomas.

was raised on their allotted lands on the north side of Miami. The following is a short excerpt about her life growing up as she remembered it: "Before Grandpa chose his home at where North Miami now stands, he lived near Peoria on what is now called the Old Skye Place....The home near Peoria was a log one, small but comfortable and I started to school at the old Peoria School House which I attended for some time but was sent from there to Haskell and later to Carlisle where I remained for three years without coming home. The climate did not agree with me but I liked it and was afraid to come home."

In 1893, Isadora married Thomas W. Smith, a Munsee Indian from Miami County, Kansas. Isadora and Thomas lived on farmland allotted to their Labadie Family that is now the G.A.R. Cemetery in Miami. Their children were Roth, Ella, Frank, Ralph, Arlice, Ruby, and Ruth. Isadora's daughters also went to boarding school while the boys helped their father on the farm. Though they were quite successful at farming, the Smith family had their share of heartache. By 1910, Isadora had given birth to eight children, but three had passed away. Their first son died when he was just a toddler, around 1900. Roth also died during childhood, at the age of 7. The family suffered a terrible tragedy when their son Frank, who was a hemophiliac, was injured and died in a farming accident at 13 years old.

In 2000, the Miami Nation established their first cultural grounds on Isadora's allotment. The land has served the community well as a place for language education through the Eewansaapita program and other community gatherings.

katakimaankwa
Frank D. Aveline
Born: about 1862 ❖ Died: 20 January 1907

The son of James Aveline and Betsy Weakse (whose Myaamia name was recorded as Wahwindemoquah), Frank became an orphan as a young boy. He was also a step-brother to Josie Geboe Fulkerson. He attended Carlisle Indian School and afterward moved to New York to work on a railroad. He never married and was working as a painter when he died in New York City in 1907.

ceenkwihšinka
Rose Ann Bertrand Mahiner Kishco Keah

Born: about 1846 ❖ Died: about 1907

The daughter of Akima Napihšinka and a Myaamia woman whose name was written as Cha-ka-sak-wah, it is believed that Rose Ann was born shortly after the removal to Kansas. Her parents never had English names, and she was not likely known by her Anglicized name of Rose Ann until an adult. She married Joseph Bertrand around 1867 and had a daughter, Madeline, who died as a toddler. Several years later she married a man whose surname was Mahiner; his given name is alternately recorded as Jack or David. Her daughter Lizzie was born after the relocation to Indian Territory but before allotments were made. Though no record of what happened to her second husband has been found, it is evident she also married a man named John (nicknamed Nephew) Kishco and had a son, Joseph. After the death of both Nephew and Joseph, Rose Ann married once more. In 1902, she was married to Joseph Keah, an Ottawa Indian. Though an official record of her death has not been found, she stops appearing in tribal records around 1907, so she likely died in 1907 or 1908.

ašiihiwia
Lizzie Mahiner Gokey

Born: 15 April 1877 ❖ Died: 11 December 1951

Lizzie was a teenager when she was allotted her land about a mile east of the Drake House. However, it wasn't long after that when she married Leo Gokey, a member of the Sac & Fox Tribe, and left her mother Rose Ann for the Sac & Fox reservation area in Lincoln County, Oklahoma. Lizzie's Myaamia lineage comes through her maternal grandfather, Napihšinka, a chief during the 1860s. Not much is known of her father David (or Jack) Mahiner, except that he was likely Potawatomi. Though she was born in Indian Territory, Lizzie attended school at Wabash, Indiana, for three years and Chilocco Indian School for four years. Lizzie and Leo had eight children who were all citizens of the Sac & Fox Nation. The two oldest, Adam and John, are pictured in the photo, followed by Amelia, Eunice, James, Rosetta, Elmer, and Minnie. Lizzie continued to live in the Stroud, Oklahoma, area for the rest of her life until she passed in 1951. Though the family was physically and paternally associated with the Sac & Fox culture, they also maintained their connection with their Myaamia heritage, and many of her descendants have elected to return to the Miami Nation as citizens.

Photo courtesy Donna Littleton

Lizzie and Leo Gokey with their children Adam, left, and John.

napihšinka
Joseph Kishco
Born: 1882 ❖ Died: 1896

Named after his grandfather, who served as a chief in Kansas following the Myaamia removal from Indiana, Joseph lived a short life of fourteen years. His family greatly mourned his passing, as evidenced by the relatively intricate marker made for his grave, which includes a cross and carved lamb. Both his and his father's graves are some of the oldest located on the eastern side of the current Myaamia tribal cemetery grounds. His final resting place is located about one mile directly north of his allotted land.

Allotment #61

Photo courtesy Pooler-McMullen Family Papers, MSI, MHMA Collection

waapimaankohkwa
Mary Louisa Richardville Pooler
Born: 24 August 1858 ❖ Died: 8 April 1928

Mary Louisa was born in Indiana, the daughter of Akima Waapimaankwa (Chief Thomas F. Richardville) and Angeline Goodboo. Along with her sister Rose Ann, she stayed with her mother's family in Indiana for several years before moving west around the time of relocation to Indian Territory. She married Manford Pooler, who would become Chief of the Ottawa Tribe. Their children, however, enrolled under the Miami Nation, and two sons, Frank and Louis were given Miami allotments. All together, Mary Louisa and Manford Pooler had eight children, two of whom died as very young children. In addition to Frank and Louis, there were Josephine, Mabel, Frederick, and Ernest.

Photo courtesy Norval Pooler, MS 11, MHMA Collection

Frank Pooler, right, with his
brother Ernest.

palaanswa
Francis C. 'Frank' Pooler

Born: 22 October 1885 ❖ Died: April 1966

Francis, who was always known by "Frank," lived his entire life in the Ottawa County area. He and his wife, Mamie Simpson, had no children of their own but raised Frank's nephew, Robert Pooler. Frank lived with a disability, having lost his right hand. He worked often assisting his father when he owned a livery business and then in odd jobs supporting the mining industry near Quapaw and Picher, Oklahoma.

Allotment #63

Louis David Pooler

Born: 18 December 1888 ❖ Died: 17 April 1910

The youngest tribal member to receive an allotment, Louis David Pooler was just starting to establish himself as a young businessman when he passed away while traveling away from home in 1910, at the age of 21. He never married nor had any children.

Photo courtesy McMain Family

maankoonsihkwa
Rose Ann Richardville Demo

Born: 6 March 1859 ❖ Died: 14 August 1907

Rose Ann Richardville, the daughter of Thomas Richardville and Angeline Goodboo (also a Myaamia woman), was born in Indiana in 1859. She lived with her mother in Indiana for most of her childhood, and joined her father in Kansas as a teenager, in about 1870. She married Joseph F. Demo, Sr., in Miami County, Kansas on May 19, 1878. She received an allotment both in Kansas and in Indian Territory. Rose Ann gave birth to three sons: Thomas (who died as a young boy), Charles, and Joseph. Charles was one of the youngest children to receive an allotment, and Joseph was born the year after allotments were concluded.

Photo courtesy Connie McMain Long

waakihšinka
Charles Marcum Demo

Born: 15 October 1887 ❖ Died: 10 October 1969

Charles Demo was part of the first generation of Myaamia born in Indian Territory. He married Mary Williss Bailey on August 8, 1909, in Miami, Oklahoma. They had two daughters, Rosie and Mary Charlene. Charlie was a leader in the community of Miami and was a life-long farmer. He lived and farmed in the area of the Myaamia allotment lands all his life. He served in many civic capacities, including treasurer for Quapaw Township, jury commissioner, member of the Ottawa County Free Fair Board, Ottawa County Soil Conservation District, Ottawa County Dairy Association, and trustee for the Northeast Oklahoma Electric Cooperative. Charlie was also active in tribal affairs throughout his lifetime. After the Tribe was organized under the 1936 Oklahoma Indian Welfare Act, Demo served on the tribal enrollment committee and also served as a Tribal Councilperson in the 1960s.

Edward Gibson Harris

Born: 9 February 1874 ❖ Died: 16 June 1941

The grandson of Akima Eecipoonkwia (Chief John B. Roubidoux), Edward's mother Sarah died directly after his birth. His father was Dr. John Harris, who left him in the care of his Myaamia relatives, namely his grandfather and aunt, Sophia Goodboo. He grew up in Indian Territory, and married Ida Belle Cornett in 1895. Together they had six children, four girls and two boys. They stayed in the Miami area for a few years after marriage before work on the railroad took them west to Oklahoma City, then on to Denver, finally settling in Portland, Oregon. Though he moved far away from his relatives, he never forgot his Myaamia roots. His son Grant was even able to travel back to his birthplace late in his life. He always made sure the younger generations of nieces and nephews knew they were Miami Indians.

Alphabetical Index of Allottees with Allotment Number

[Women listed by maiden name]

Numerical Index of Allottees by Allotment Number

1	John Miller
2	Esther Miller Dagenett
3	Lewis W. Miller
4	David Geboe
5	Mary Bridget Leonard Geboe
6	Minnie Geboe Trinkle
7	Oscar LaFalier
8	Henry LaFalier
9	Mary 'Necy' LaFalier Gobin
10	David LaFalier
11	Jessie LaFalier Youngblood
12	William 'Wayne' Drake
13	Louisa Drake Roseberry
14	Lucy Josephine 'Josie' Geboe Paup Fulkerson
15	Mary Louise Roubidoux Leonard
16	Jane Pigeon Drake
17	Mary Drake VanDusen
18	Josephine 'Josie' Drake Pope
19	David H. Drake
20	Edward Drake
21	Sarah Drake Horton
22	Milton D. Drake, Jr.
23	John L. Drake
24	Thomas S. Drake
25	Martha 'Marchie' Drake Hale Runkle
26	Mary Adeline Boure Dollar Billington
27	Theodore W. Dollar
28	Silver 'Luddie' Dollar Lucas
29	Adeline G. Billington Leonard
30	Milton Howard Billington
31	Margaret 'Peggy' Davis Bright
32	John L. Bright
33	Florence 'Flora' Bright

34	Columbus Bright
35	George W. Leonard
36	Charles W. Leonard
37	Helen Leonard Sims
38	Barbara 'Anna' Leonard Murray Schultz
39	Louisa Geboe Leonard
40	Thomas F. Richardville
41	Mary Lindsey Richardville
42	Hannah Richardville McManaman
43	Catherine Richardville Simpson
44	Charles W. Richardville
45	Lizzie Lindsey Palmer
46	Thomas 'Harley' Palmer
47	Charles S. Welch
48	Sophia Roubidoux Bluejacket Goodboo LaFalier
49	Mary Shapp Wea Buck Daugherty
50	Frank Buck, Jr.
51	Susan Crawfish
52	Luella Isadore Crawfish Beaver Quapaw Wilson
53	Peter Shapp
54	Lizzie Davis Thompson McCoontz
55	Susan Benjamin Medicine
56	Isadora Labadie Smith
57	Frank D. Aveline
58	Rose Ann Bertrand Mahiner Kishco Keah
59	Lizzie Mahiner Gokey
60	Joseph Kishco
61	Mary Louise Richardville Pooler
62	Francis C. 'Frank' Pooler
63	Louis David Pooler
64	Rose Ann Richardville Demo
65	Charles M. Demo
66	Edward G. Harris

Index of Family Groups

[Allotment number in parentheses]

Aveline: Frank D. Aveline (57)

Billington-Dollar: Mary Adeline Boure Dollar Billington (26)
                        Adeline G. Billington Leonard (29)
                        Milton Howard Billington (30)
                        Silver 'Luddie' Dollar Lucas (28)
                        Theodore W. Dollar (27)

Bright: Columbus Bright (34)
                        Florence 'Flora' Bright (33)
                        John L. Bright (32)
                        Margaret Peggy Davis Bright (31)

Davis: Lizzie Davis Thompson McCoontz (54)

Drake: Jane Pigeon Drake (16)
                        David H. Drake (19)
                        Edward Drake (20)
                        John L. Drake (23)
                        Josephine 'Josie' Drake Pope (18)
                        Louisa Drake Roseberry (13)
                        Martha 'Marchie' Drake Hale Runkle (25)
                        Mary Drake VanDusen (17)
                        Milton Drake, Jr. (22)
                        Sarah Drake Horton (21)
                        Thomas S. Drake (24)
                        William 'Wayne' Drake (12)

Geboe: David Geboe (4)
                        Mary Bridget Leonard Geboe (5)
                        Minnie Geboe Trinkle (6)
                        Lucy Josephine 'Josie' Geboe Paup Fulkerson (14)
                        Louisa Geboe Leonard (39)

Mahiner-Kishco: Rose Ann Bertrand Mahiner Kishco Keah (58)
                        Lizzie Mahiner Gokey (59)
                        Joseph Kishco (60)

Labadie: Isadora Labadie Smith (56)

LaFalier:	David LaFalier (10)
	Henry LaFalier (8)
	Jessie LaFalier Youngblood (11)
	Mary 'Necy' LaFalier Gobin (9)
	Oscar LaFalier (7)

Leonard:
Barbara 'Anna' Leonard Murray Schultz (38)
Charles W. Leonard (36)
George W. Leonard (35)
Helen Leonard Sims (37)
Mary Louise Roubidoux Leonard (15)

Miller:
John Miller (1)
Lewis W. Miller (3)
Esther Miller Dagenett (2)
Susan Benjamin Medicine (55)

Richardville:
Thomas F. Richardville (40)
Mary Lindsey Richardville (41)
Lizzie Lindsey Palmer (45)
Thomas 'Harley' Palmer (46)
Rose Ann Richardville Demo (64)
Charles M. Demo (65)
Mary Louise Richardville Pooler (61)
Francis C. 'Frank' Pooler (62)
Louis David Pooler (63)
Hannah Richardville McManaman (42)
Catherine Richardville Simpson (43)
Charles W. Richardville (44)

Roubidoux:
Sophia Roubidoux Goodboo LaFalier (48)
Edward G. Harris (66)

Shapp:
Susan Crawfish (51)
Luella Isadore Crawfish Beaver Quapaw Wilson (52)
Mary Shapp Wea Buck Daugherty (49)
Frank Buck, Jr. (50)
Peter Shapp (53)

Welch:
Charles S. Welch (47)

About the Contributors

George Ironstrack has participated in Myaamia language renewal projects as both a student and a teacher since the mid-1990s. Originally from Chicago, George, Tamise, and their children Kai, Mirin, and Jordi all make their home in Oxford, OH. George is a citizen of the Miami Tribe of Oklahoma and has assisted in the organization and administration of the Tribe's Eewansaapita Summer Educational Experience since its inception in 2005. George received an M.A. in Origins and History of the United States from the Department of History at Miami University in 2006. His graduate work centered on the Miami Indian village of Pickawillany, which was located in western Ohio near the city of Piqua. George continues to regularly research and write about Myaamia history. In 2008, George joined the Myaamia Center at Miami University (myaamiacenter.org) as its Assistant Director and currently heads up the Center's Education & Outreach Office. Examples of his work can be found on the Myaamia Community History & Ecology Blog: Aacimotaatiiyankwi (myaamiahistory.wordpress.com). As both a tribal educator and a former public school teacher, George is also interested in the study of indigenous pedagogical practices and specifically Myaamia Neepwaantiinki (Miami Education).

Meghan Dorey has worked for the Myaamia Heritage Museum and Archive at the Miami Tribe of Oklahoma since its opening in 2007. She graduated from the University of Minnesota, Morris, with a bachelor's degree in Social Sciences in 2005, and the University of Wisconsin, Milwaukee, School of Information Studies with a Masters of Library and Information Science in 2007. Born and raised in rural Minnesota, Meghan relocated to Oklahoma to join the staff of the Miami Tribe of Oklahoma. She was promoted to Manager of the Myaamia Heritage Museum & Archive in 2015, where she oversees the preservation of and access to historical records and objects of enduring value to the Miami Nation. She and her husband, tribal citizen Matthew Dorey, reside in Miami, Oklahoma, with their sons Jensen and Josiah.

Bradford Kasberg has worked under the Cultural Resources Office of the Miami Tribe of Oklahoma as a Special Projects Researcher since 2012. He supports work regarding historical and modern mapping, ecological planning, and the design and ecological restoration of properties owned by the Miami Tribe. As a citizen of the Miami Tribe of Oklahoma he also assists in language support in tribal educational programs. He graduated from Miami University in 2012 with a Bachelors of Arts in Geography and Anthropology. Upon graduation he was awarded the Joanna J. Goldman Prize, a research grant supporting his research integrating Myaamia traditional ecological knowledge and the potential for associated risks of community health in areas of environmental contamination. He recently graduated from the University of Michigan with a Masters of Landscape Architecture.